THE GOD WHO
DARED

THE GOD WHO DARED

Genesis:
From Creation to Babel

DOUGLAS JACOBY

One Merrill Street
Woburn, MA 01801
1-888-DPI-BOOK Fax (617) 937-3889

The God Who Dared
©1997 by Discipleship Publications International
One Merrill Street, Woburn, MA 01801

Printed in the United States of America

Cover design: Chris Costello
Interior design: Chris Costello and Laura Root

ISBN 1-57782-002-9

From his first knock on my door Douglas Arthur was to change the course of my life forever. His friendship and family taught me how to be a friend, inspired me to marry and to raise a family. His determination to make an impact on the world inspired me to become an evangelist and teacher. His effectiveness in communicating and keen sensitivity to the black and white (and gray) of truth totally transformed how I think and write. More than any other person, Douglas Arthur has helped me to grasp the heart of God.

Of course, the debt to my friend of twenty years cannot be boiled down to a hundred words, but I am able to dedicate this book to him.

Contents

Introduction

Daring to Write

Since the book of Genesis is where Bible readers often begin, the first impression it creates is incredibly important. I sense intuitively that more than sheer coincidence has placed Genesis at the head of the biblical books—just as Revelation is perfectly positioned, not just accidentally, to close the canon of Scripture.

The book that God uses to begin his written revelation to man must be handled carefully and reverently. In Genesis the true heart of God—his nature and his plan for man and woman—spills over onto the sacred pages. We have a close encounter of the most significant kind as we meet the LORD of the universe.

Natural Apprehension

I have read hundreds of books and articles on Genesis in the last twenty years, sometimes to prepare myself to answer other people's questions, often to answer my own! In fact, my fascination since my high school years with the subject matter of Genesis—life, meaning, origins, destiny—prepared me for conversion as a college student. As an eager freshman with fire in his eyes, a yearning in his heart and time on his hands, I grabbed and read everything I could find that might address the things I wondered about: cosmology, biology, evolutionary science and so on.

Today as a lecturer (still eager, though with less time on

his hands!) I speak endlessly on these matters (so it seems), take questions from the floor, and handle quite a large correspondence annually from inquirers the world over. Many questions concern the early chapters of Genesis. Although I have written a good number of books and articles, and usually feel quite comfortable taking up a theme and elaborating on it, I must confess I feel a certain apprehension in approaching Genesis. Will I, as author, accurately convey the truth about Genesis, or simply throw one more well-meaning but misguided interpretation into the theological vortex?

It takes courage to address the knotty issues—some of the scientific questions Genesis raises, for example. Then there's the challenge of practical exegesis. The word of God must enter our hearts and lives to be implemented daily. Will I illuminate the text accurately, or succumb to the temptation to import my own agenda? I am vaguely lulled from my pursuit by the thought of Psalm 131 ("My heart is not proud, O LORD, my eyes are not haughty; I do not concern myself with great matters or things too wonderful for me"), while haunted by the words of Job 40:4-5 and 42:3-6:

> *"I am unworthy—how can I reply to you?*
> *I put my hand over my mouth.*
> *I spoke once, but I have no answer—*
> *twice, but I will say no more....*
> *Surely I spoke of matters I did not understand,*
> *things too wonderful for me to know....*
> *My ears had heard of you,*
> *but now my eyes have seen you.*
> *Therefore I despise myself*
> *and repent in dust and ashes."*

Yet, like Jeremiah, I find I can no longer contain the overwhelming desire to speak clearly, to face the press and to take a stand (Jeremiah 20:9). So much nonsense about Genesis has been taught in the name of God! But the vast majority of men and women on the planet still don't know the Lord, and confused teaching does not help the situation. Besides this, the constant pressure and prejudice of the world daily makes thousands of Jesus' disciples ashamed, fearful that they have no answers to the questions (and even jeers) of the "unbelieving generation" (Mark 9:19).

And so I dare to write this book, and I pray that God will use it for his kingdom and correct me where I may have gone wrong. The basic teachings of Genesis certainly come to light quickly, and they are beyond dispute. However, there are a few matters of opinion (Romans 14:1), and I realize that brothers and sisters of sound mind and good spiritual heart may take exception to some teachings advanced in this book. I do not look down on them, yet I do ask them to defend their reasoning where they differ.

Yes, the book needed writing, and I can delay no longer. For, in the words of Jeremiah the prophet, "I am weary of holding it in; indeed, I cannot" (Jeremiah 20:9).

The God Who Dared

This volume covers chapters 1-11 of Genesis. I have entitled it *The God Who Dared: Creation to Babel*, because it is here that God discloses his heart to man—a heart that dared to first create, then "re-create." A second volume to be published later, *The God Who Dared: Abraham to Egypt* will cover the remainder of Genesis (chapters 12-50) and will trace the spiritual journeys of men and women of faith from Abraham and Sarah to Joseph. This two-volume project grew out of a series taught in the British Isles where my wife and I served in the ministry in 1995-96.

In this book I wanted to accent the true heart of the Old Testament, which is so often misrepresented as dealing with spiritual matters in a superficial, external way, or in a manner somehow inferior to the New Testament. Those who would detract from the Old Testament should realize first that this was the Bible of the early Christians and of Jesus himself! (Romans 15:4; 1 Corinthians 10:11; 2 Timothy 3:15-17; Luke 24:44-45). The whole Bible is God's word, and it all starts with Genesis.

The Fast Track

This book contains a number of endnotes, not to mention all the extra material in the Appendixes. Some readers may prefer to read straight through and skip the endnotes and appendixes. Certainly they will finish the book more quickly, and perhaps on another reading they will want to wade through every note and appendix. This is the "fast track."

Other readers, however, may not want to miss anything the first time through. In any case, there are two tracks, as well as combinations of the two, which all have their advantages. You decide which course you would like to plot!

Deep Darkness, Burning Beacon

Our world has a desperate, felt need for God. It is in Genesis that God begins to reveal himself, and we must teach from Genesis to fully cut through the deep darkness (Proverbs 4:19). As we approach the new millennium, thinking men and women demand clear answers. They desperately seek a beacon to guide them through the thick darkness of a society beset by the clanging emptiness of technology, the disillusionment of shattered relationships, and the deep confusion of a world cut loose from its moral moorings—spinning its way into oblivion. The word of God is that beacon, and it is in Genesis that the torch first bursts into flame!

Doug Jacoby
Chevy Chase, Maryland
September, 1996

DARING IN CREATION

*God's dazzling, daring creation involved
preparing a planet for population. Risking personal heart-
break, he set the earth spinning with
a creature called "human" walking its surface. His plan was
perfect, yet not without certain risks, as we shall see in
Section II. God dared to create.*

1
Shaking Hands with God

God's Personal Introduction

In the Bible God has so much to tell us—about himself, about ourselves, about his plan for us—and only some thousand pages in which to record his will, our destiny and his heart. God speaks; the question is, "Who's listening?"

The Book

Now a thousand pages may seem like a great amount. Yet the same people who complain about the substantial length of the Bible often manage to find time each year to read thousands upon thousands of pages of novels, magazines and literature of dubious value. They sit mindlessly in front of a television set for countless hours per week—for what? If we really understood that the infinite God has put his vital message in a book so thin, so compact and convenient, we would thank him!

So many people start reading the Bible, and then stop. It's more than their "busy" schedules or need for a tutor that causes them to freeze in their tracks. They feel, almost instinctively, that in this book there is something chillingly different from us and our nature. For us sinners there is something terrifying about the holy, something eerily transcendent and at the same time unsettling and comforting, something we hide from, yet something which we desperately need. Something that, if allowed to, would radically change our lives—for the good!

This isn't just another religious book. It is *the* Book of all books.

Shaking Hands with God

In the collection of writings known as the Bible,[1] Genesis stands as the introduction—the LORD's introduction to his message to man. In the divine play in which all of us have a role, be it major or minor, Genesis is Act I, Scene 1. Here the plot begins to unfold and all subplots are set in motion, if only embryonically. Every essential theme of the Bible is elaborated in Genesis.

This book is the introduction not only to the Bible as a whole, but also to the heart and soul of God and his perfect, practical plans for mankind. To read Genesis is to shake hands with God.

When we first meet someone, we form an impression. In my life I have shaken hands with celebrities, politicians and athletes. Some made a great first impression; for others the same, unfortunately, cannot be said. But we usually remember that first encounter. I recall meeting Gary Knutson with his black boots and intense eyes, and Douglas Arthur,[2] bearded and easygoing, as they knocked on my dormitory door and invited me to a Bible discussion. Little did they know how receptive I really was, in my heart.

So it is when we first really meet God. The impression is powerful, unforgettable, enduring. His heart comes out clearly in Genesis.

Excursus on the Word *Genesis*

Genesis is the Greek word for "beginning, origin or descent,"[3] and appropriately describes the situation in which mankind finds itself: God began it all, we have our origin in his person and will, and every generation is descended from him.[4] Jewish tradition holds that Moses either wrote or was responsible for the whole Pentateuch (the five rolls, or Torah).[5] Accordingly, in some translations, like the German and the Swedish, Genesis is called "The First Book of Moses," while

other tongues, like French and Spanish, use an equivalent of
"Genesis."

Genesis and Generations

The book of Genesis is a carefully constructed work. At
the simplest level it may be divided into two sections:[6] the
primeval period and the patriarchal period.[7] The outline con-
sists of four events in the primeval age and then four main
characters in the patriarchal age.

Primeval Period	Patriarchal Period
Adam and Eve (Garden)	Abraham (11:27-25:18)
Cain and Abel (Field)	Isaac[8] (21:1-35:29)
Noah and Family (Flood)	Jacob (25:19-37:1)
Group and Babel (Tower)	Joseph (37:2-50:26)

At a deeper level it is soon seen that Genesis is constructed
around ten "generations." Other biblical works also follow a
structural theme: Matthew is built around five tracts of teaching material,[9] while Lamentations is an acrostic poem.[10] Not
all English translations preserve the Hebrew word "generations," so don't get disillusioned if you have trouble tracing
the theme in your favorite Bible! The Generations theme defines the purposes of the book of Genesis.[11] Clearly the author is tracing the "chosen seed of Israel's race,"—that is, the
generations of the chosen people, the Jews—genealogically
from the first man on down.

Life is not random, nor does it meander like some dreamy
stream. It is directional, and fraught with meaning and purpose. To discover our origin is to discover our destiny.

Generations

We see that Genesis is not primarily a book about cosmology (the study of the universe), cosmogony (the origin of
the universe) or biogenesis (the generation of life). (See Appendix B for more about science and the Bible.) The Genera-

tions of Genesis do have almost completely to do with *people,*
not protons, protoplasm or pulsars. It's not that biology, chemistry and physics aren't important. It's just that they don't help
us with the purpose of life, and unless we get a handle on the
heart of God, they scarcely even improve the quality of our
lives.

The Ten Generations (*toledoth* in Hebrew)[12] are as follows:

1. The Heavens and the earth (Genesis 2:4a)
2. Adam and his descendants (5:1)
3. Noah (6:9)
4. Ham, Shem and Japheth (10:1)
5. Shem (11:10)
6. Terah (11:27)
7. Ishmael (25:12)
8. Isaac (25:19)
9. Esau (36:1)
10. Jacob[13] (37:2)

The 50 chapters of Genesis present the Creation in hardly
more than 50 verses. The focus rapidly narrows from "the
heavens and the earth" to the creation of mankind in the first
family, and then continues to narrow along the genealogy that
leads, ultimately (and in the next testament) to the birth of
the Savior of the world. Truly Genesis is a book of origins!

Twelve Themes

Genesis is where God spells out *how life works*—no, not
the super-complex mechanisms of microbiology, but meaningful life on this planet as God intended it. The major themes
of Genesis are, in short, the major themes of the Bible. They
are the most important principles for living life to the full! In
them the very heart of God is articulated.

1. *God* - He is the Creator, and human beings enjoy "most

favored creature status." God does not beg for our service, nor does he require worship out of insecurity. His blessings toward us do not flow from some need on his part, but rather from the wellspring of his kindness and initiative. Outside the Bible no "god" is so personal and eagerly desirous of a personal relationship with his creatures. Whereas the world teaches that we are not individually special, God strongly disagrees!

2. *Worship* - We can worship only one God. Other gods are false gods. Once again, worship is for our benefit, not his. We are the primary beneficiaries!

3. *Order* - God is a God of order, his creation is good, and he is consistently reasonable. The Lord is not whimsical, sadistic or erratic. His heart is good, and for each of us to have a good heart, we need to be in submission to the order established by God.

4. *Sin and Guilt* - Morality is real and sin is at the root of our problems, directly or indirectly. Sin breaks the heart of God (Genesis 6:6).

5. *Sacrifice* - True religion is based on true sacrifice. God requires sacrifice of us, just as he is a God of sacrifice, always giving his best, never holding back. Moreover, God cannot be manipulated by sacrifice. We don't control God, God controls us!

6. *Grace* - God is always willing to give us a fresh start! What a heart our Creator has! Grace is one of the strongest themes in Genesis, as we shall see in a later chapter.

7. *Providence* - God provides for his creation, anticipating a need years—even generations—in advance and working out the details for it to be met.

8. *Marriage and Family* - God's normal plan for our happiness is marriage and family. If we do things God's way, these relationships bring blessings. Depart from his plan and enter rough waters indeed!

9. *Work* - Man is created to work, not to be lazy. The institu-

tion of work (surprisingly) predates the Fall, being present in the condition of "paradise"!

10. *Justice* - Crime must be requited with punishment. Or conversely, as Gilbert and Sullivan put it, "Let the punishment fit the crime." Sin is sin, no matter how much we rationalize it or talk about motives or "goodwill." A sense of justice runs deep and strong in the Old Testament. We all share this conviction: God must be fair.

11. *Seed* - This is closely connected with the Generations theme. We can trace the theme from the seed of Eve through Abraham, Isaac, Jacob and Judah—on the way to the Messiah. God, faithful to his promises, jealously protects his chosen seed, and is unwilling to tolerate those who would extinguish the line of his godly offspring. (See especially Genesis 38.)

12. *Covenant* - The heart of God longs for friendship with man, but on certain terms in a covenant relationship (Genesis 9, 15, 17, 28). If we fulfill our part, then God fulfills his. Yet this is hardly a relationship among equals! God is virtually 100% the benefactor, and we virtually 100% the beneficiaries.

We approach each of these themes correctly or incorrectly every day depending on whether we have a scriptural perspective—all the more reason to make every effort to get God's perspective! Moreover, many of these themes are assumed, or taken for granted, later on in the Bible. (Have you ever noticed how many of them are worked into the warp and woof of the Scriptures?) God laid things out very clearly, and he did so in *his* introduction to his book, where his heart is made manifest.

God in Heaven, Man in a Coffin

Life is short. On your tombstone, there will be two dates separated by a dash. That dash is your life![14] Our decisions carry eternal weight and God's voice must be heard. His word is the Bible, and Genesis is the introduction. We can't afford to miss it! Missing the first ten minutes of a movie may mean we never do figure out the plot. We may think the bad guy is the good guy, or we aren't sure the good guy isn't a bad guy after all. When we skip the beginning of a book, we miss something. So it is with Genesis. *Attendez-vous, achtung, listen up!* We definitely don't want to miss a word.

We need to be humble. We need to be good listeners. We mustn't rush through the word of God, but rather strain to catch his every word. As has been aptly remarked, Genesis begins with God in heaven and ends with man in a coffin (Genesis 1:1, 50:26).

We will do well to listen to our Creator's voice, cherish his heart, and prepare ourselves in this life to meet our God.

Notes

1. It is clear when you look at its history that the word *Bible* was not originally a religious word. It comes simply from the Greek *ta biblia* (the books), which comes in turn from *biblos/bublos* (scroll or paper). Most of the earliest books (examples of what paleographers call the *Codex*) were Bibles. The fact that we even have books flows largely from the conviction of the early Christians that the books of the Bible were the word of God and were to be published for all to read, hear and understand.

2. To whom this book is dedicated.

3. *A Greek-English Lexicon of The New Testament and Other Early Christian Literature,* F.W. Gingrich and Frederick Danker, University of Chicago Press, 1979. This is one of the easiest reference books about how Greek words were used in early Christian times. Greek must be seen as a language in evolution, as must all languages. A word in classical Greek (the fourth century B.C.) often had changed significantly by NT times—and the change in meaning in modern Greek is often more dramatic still. For example, *psallo* (the verb related to the noun *psalm*) originally meant "touch, stir, or move by touching; pull, pluck; twang with the fingers." In the absolute it meant "to play" and later "to sing to a harp." In the third century B.C., Septuagint Greek *psallo* rarely meant "play," but rather "sing." NT Greek had indeed changed considerably since classical times: *psallo* meant "sing" or "sing praise." Finally, in modern Greek *psallo* means "sing" exclusively. It has lost completely its original sense of instrumental accompaniment.

4. The word *genesis* is related to the word for birth (*gennesis,* notice the extra 'n'), in Greek as well as in the original Hebrew. In English we call this book, as we do many biblical books, by the Greek name. In Hebrew, the original language of 98% of the Old Testament, it is called B'*re'shith,* which is actually the first word of the Bible, literally meaning "in the beginning."

5. How much of them he actually penned is a matter, in my opinion, for the experts to hash out.

6. This is the approach most commentaries take, and it is a natural enough way to begin the study of Genesis.

7. Use of the term "primeval" in no way implies this period is fictional. Primeval means "pertaining to the first age of the world; primitive" (Oxford Abridged Dictionary). A "patriarch" is "a father and ruler of a family or tribe," hence the term "patriarchal."

8. Compared to Abraham, Jacob and Joseph, Isaac noticeably plays quite a minor (though important) role.

9. Paralleling, in all likelihood, the five books of the Torah; Matthew gives the "new" law.

10. That is, each successive verse begins with the next letter of the Hebrew alphabet. For an even more striking example, see Psalm 119; even if you can't read Hebrew, you will easily see the repetition of letters at the beginning of each line.

11. Many theologians have found an even deeper inner structure in the flow of Genesis, but this is beyond the scope of this book.

12. If you search for this word in a scholarly computer program [such as Hermeneutika's *BibleWorks for Windows*, (406) 837-2244] you will notice that the Hebrew text can be confusing. The ten *toledoth* passages spell the word *toledoth* three different ways! (Without the vowels, *twldth*, 6x; *tldwth*, 3x; and *twldwth*, 1x!)

13. Two important notes here: first, the repetition of the *ten* motif, as in the ten generations from Adam to Noah and the ten from Noah to Abram; second, the absence of Abraham and Joseph from the *toledoth* formula, since their lives take up such a substantial part of the book.

As for Abraham, Terah's line included not just Abraham but a large number of the personae of Genesis, men and women who are important characters in Genesis. As for Joseph, keeping in mind that Genesis is written for Jews and from a Jewish perspective, it is proper that the ten generations not go beyond Jacob, the father of the twelve tribes. In this way, the accent is left on Jacob's generation—Israel—thus setting the stage for the Exodus, which, after all, involved more than the tribes of Ephraim and Manasseh.

14. Or, as John Lennon put it, "Life is what happens to you while you are making other plans."

2
C:\CREATION.EXE

Day One

We begin our study of Genesis with the familiar creation account. What may not be familiar is that God *dared* to create. This was no gamble in the human sense—transacted with uncertainty as to the outcome—yet there was still the element of risk. It takes daring to create, especially where a world of delicately balanced relationships is involved.

God gave a simple command. In our computer-conscious age, it might have been typed C:\CREATION.EXE. There is no question that when God hit the "enter" key, it was an executable command. The program ran. The cosmos was created. Life began.

Now the Creation account may seem too simple, too shallow to speak meaningfully to our age. Genesis is dismissed as irrelevant by many of our younger people—the video generation, the MTV crowd, Generation 'X.' Or it is dismissed as simplistic by the well educated, and by men and women (educated or not) who enjoy thinking and asking questions. Yet, as we shall see, in the very first verse of God's word we find something that today eludes many of the brightest minds of our world.

> *1:1In the beginning God created the heavens and the earth. 2Now the earth was formless and empty, darkness was over the surface of the deep, and the Spirit of God was hovering over the waters.*

The Beginning

Modern man, in the pursuit of meaning and in his quest for his true origins, is at a total loss as to how to explain the mystery of life. How did inanimate matter lead to life, according to the full-blown theory of evolution, and human life in particular? The question is, just how did *human life* come to be? Why are we so similar to some animals yet so very different from them all? What is the source of our self-consciousness, reflection on life, spiritual instinct and other qualities never found in the rest of the biological world?

This is a white-hot topic, usually at the top of the list in scientific discussions these days. It's right up there with Could dinosaurs be cloned from fossil DNA?; Does global warming threaten the earth?; and Does the Antarctic meteor prove life evolved on Mars?

The answer is found here, in Genesis 1: "In the beginning [was] *God*" (emphasis added). Verse 1 tells us that God has always been. He requires no creator (as though he were material!), but is himself the absolute initiator of the universe. There will never be a valid explanation for humanity—mankind's free will, heart and personality—if God is left out of the picture.[1] The Bible tells us not only that God was in the picture (at the beginning), but that he in fact *drew* the picture![2]

This is no children's story. Contrary to popular belief, when we go to Genesis, we leave the world of mythology and enter the world of reality! Even when mythical terms or concepts are borrowed, they are turned on their head, thus showing the bankruptcy of the confusion of paganism.

The world was "formless and empty," (1:2) as well as dark. Yet darkness gives way to light, chaos to cosmos.[3] The Spirit of God hovers over the surface of the *waters* (a common symbol for chaos in the Bible, as well as in ancient religions). Something is about to happen. This is always the way with the Spirit of God![4]

Trick Question: *Who Made God?*

Sometimes someone asks, "Who made God?" The question is really inappropriate, since *by definition* God has no maker; he is uncaused, outside space and time. Like the question Have you stopped beating your wife?, this contains a hidden premise, rejecting the possibility that there *is* a God—just as the other question refuses to consider the innocence of the man in question. You might as well ask, "What does *loud silence* sound like?" This, too, is inappropriate, since silence *by definition* cannot be noisy. Yet the question isn't surprising, since modern man has forgotten who God is. He has forgotten what absolutes are; definitions these days seem up for grabs.

Genesis 1:1-3 is especially dynamic in the Fox translation:

> At the beginning of God's creating of the heavens and the
> earth,
>   when the earth was wild and waste,
> darkness over the face of Ocean,
>   rushing-spirit of God hovering over the face of the
>   waters—
> God said: Let there be light!
> And there was light.[5]

It wasn't just the cosmos that was formless and empty before the work of the transforming hand of God. It is the same with our lives. Before we understand who God is and what Jesus Christ has done, our lives are "without form"—lacking the structure and clearly defined boundaries necessary to have real security—and "empty" (Ecclesiastes 2:17; 1 Peter 1:18).

Like the Athenian philosophers (Acts 17:21), we spend much time discussing all the latest theories without really seeing the big picture. Like the proconsul Gallio (Acts 18:17), we fail to show real compassion toward our fellow man; we are paralyzed by apathy. And like the mindless mob in Ephesus (Acts 19:32), we don't even know why we are here on this planet. Questions that most leave to the philosophers of the age, like What is truth? can receive no satisfactory answer apart from God, nor can common questions like What is my purpose in life?; or Am I significant in the scheme of things, or alone, empty and meaningless? Quite simply, life without God does not make sense![6]

Two details in 1:1-2 deserve some attention. First, the "heavens" are all of space from the surface of the earth upward (outward). In Hebrew, as in many languages, the words for "heaven" and "sky" are identical. Second, the Spirit of God was hovering over the waters, brooding like a bird.[7] In the same way, the Spirit's descent "as a dove," a bird, on Jesus (Mark 1:10) demonstrates that a *new* creation was about to begin! (2 Corinthians 5:17).

The presence of the Spirit paves the way for a later understanding of the triune nature of God—though it's unlikely the writer had this in mind as he wrote. At any rate, the stage is set; in a moment the ultimate authority in the cosmos will speak.

> [3]And God said, "Let there be light," and there was light. [4]God saw that the light was good, and he separated the light from the darkness. [5]God called the light "day," and the darkness he called "night." And there was evening, and there was morning—the first day.

God speaks. He speaks authoritatively, simply, directly. He speaks light into existence: "Let there be light."[8] Is this the Big Bang of twentieth-century cosmology? Was this the massive explosion that set the worlds in motion? Probably not, since we already find matter, energy, time and space in 1:1.[9] Was it the start of the rotation of the earth, thus creating day and night? Are we sure there was a big bang? The theory of the Big Bang doesn't remove God from the scene; it merely attempts to make sense of the fact that the entire universe is in motion.[10] Although Genesis is not a science book, many scientific questions do arise. Modern man asks questions and needs answers. (See Appendix B, "Science and Religion: Friends or Enemies?")

The Six Days of Creation

The creation days (not time!) began in 1:5. Nor did creation necessarily begin on Day One because there was already something there, according to 1:1-2.

The subtitle of this chapter is "Day One." There is a reason for this: Most translators in early centuries rendered the Hebrew *yom echad* as "day one," whereas the following days were translated "the second day, the third day," etc. In other words, this isn't just the first day of the Creation Week, but the first day ever! It was the absolute beginning of God's daring creation.[11]

Notes

1. An equation could be written: Time ("the beginning") + personality ("God") + energy ("created") + space + matter ("heavens & earth") → man. To reduce it purely to symbols, $T + \heartsuit + E + S + M \to \mathcal{O}^{7}/\mathcal{Q}$! But the physicist who is an atheist cannot possibly solve this equation and the riddle of life because he's missing one of the initial components of the universe: the very heart ($\heartsuit$) of God. His defective equation unfortunately reads: $T + E + S + M \to \mathcal{O}^{7}/\mathcal{Q}$?

2. In Genesis we see that God exists prior to and independently of the world. This is in stark contrast to other ancient cosmologies, in which the gods are hardly an improved version of man! They have little, if any, power to create. We will see in Appendix C how the original readers of Genesis would have understood the author's total refusal to give credit to the gods and goddesses—the controllers of the imaginary world of false religion.

3. The Greek *chaos* means "disorder or space," while *kosmos* is the word for "order, decoration, or world."

4. The doctrine of the Holy Spirit is not fully revealed until the New Testament. The Hebrew *ruah*, like the Greek *pneuma,* has a triple meaning: "breath, wind, spirit."

5. Everett Fox, in *The Schocken Bible, Volume I: The Five Books of Moses*, New York: Schocken Books, 1995. This is definitely an English translation with a Semitic feel! At press date only Volume I has been published.

6. Two books I highly recommend on this topic are *A Shattered Visage: The Real Face of Atheism*, and *Can Man Live Without God?* both by Ravi Zacharias (Grand Rapids: Baker Books 1990, 1994).

7. Some translations render *ruah 'elohim* as *a mighty wind*–which is possible, but unlikely in this context.

8. This is sometimes called *fiat* creation, literally "let it/there be," from the Latin *fieri* (become). Fiat creation is creation by decree.

9. Unless verses 3-5 are an amplification of verse 1. If this is the case, then an inconceivable amount of light suddenly appeared—which was tantamount to the creation of the heavens and earth.

10. As for the Big Bang, the evidence for a primordial explosion is overwhelming. Earlier this century astronomers observed the "red shift," which is a sort of Doppler Effect applied to the electromagnetic spectrum. Simply put, stars at the edge of the universe are moving at velocities approaching the speed of light (about 300,000 kilometers per second, or 186,000 mph), while star systems closer to us are receding at much lower velocities. This is exactly what happens in an explosion: the matter thrown farthest is traveling at the greatest velocity. Since gravity varies inversely as the distance between objects, the further bits of matter in the Big Bang were propelled away from the center of the universe, the less those bits would be affected by its gravitational pull, simultaneously maintaining a higher velocity and pushing back the frontiers of "space."

Despite the compelling evidence for an original explosion, estimated by most scientists to have occurred sometime in the past 15 billion years, the chance that this would have spontaneously created order (reversing the normal entropic effect of explosions) is slim. The probability that the Big Bang would have led to life is effectively nil.

11. Several English versions translate *yom echad* in Genesis 1:5 to reflect the "day one" possibility. The NAS (New American Standard) reads, "...And there was evening and there was morning, one day." The LXX Greek reads, "...day one" (*hemera mia*). Similarly, the Latin Vulgate reads "...day one" (*dies unus*). The original does technically read "day one" (*yom echad*), but it must be said that placing the cardinal number "one" (*echad*) after the noun is the normal way of expressing the ordinal "first" in Hebrew. Hence we can only conclude that the evidence is ambivalent.

3
Good, Very Good!
Days Two to Six

> [6]*And God said, "Let there be an expanse between the waters to separate water from water." [7]So God made the expanse and separated the water under the expanse from the water above it. And it was so. [8]God called the expanse "sky." And there was evening, and there was morning—the second day.*

Now we come to the second day. On the first day the light of God vanquished the eternal night; light was separated from darkness. On the second day God created the "expanse." What exactly is this "expanse" (or "firmament," to use the King James Version) separating water from water? It's the sky. Significantly, Near Eastern (a term almost interchangable with Middle Eastern) cosmology usually thought of the sky as a hard dome over a flat, disk-shaped earth.[1] (That is, the firmament was *firm*.) In Leviticus 26:19 the sky is *compared* to the hardness of iron, not necessarily *asserted* to be firm. An interesting verse in this discussion is Job 26:7, which states that the earth is suspended over nothing. This seems to be a genuine cosmological insight! The waters above the "expanse" (1:7) are evidently clouds.

> [9]*And God said, "Let the water under the sky be gathered to one place, and let dry ground appear." And it was so. [10]God called the dry ground "land," and the gathered waters he called "seas." And God saw that it was good.*

> [11]*Then God said, "Let the land produce vegetation: seed-bearing plants and trees on the land that bear fruit with seed in it, according to their various kinds." And it was so.* [12]*The land produced vegetation: plants bearing seed according to their kinds and trees bearing fruit with seed in it according to their kinds. And God saw that it was good.* [13]*And there was evening, and there was morning—the third day.*

On the third day the sea is formed and also the dry land. Geologists who specialize in plate tectonics (which concerns the drift of the continents over the eons) have demonstrated that originally the continents were joined together in one land mass.

Later on the third day God creates plants.[2] They are designed to reproduce "according to their various kinds" (1:11). The term "kinds" (*min* in Hebrew), does not mean "species." I mention this because obviously, if a kind is a species, then according to this passage, reproduction could never lead to a new species. That would imply (against all the evidence) that God created *all* species simultaneously, even that men and dinosaurs coexisted (good evening Fred Flintstone). A process of creative activity is much more in line with the evidence.

Yet the Genesis writer is discussing God's wisdom in creation and the natural world, not species, genus or genetics! The principle in this context is not the fixity of species, but reproduction (fruitfulness).

Plant life first appears on "the third day." The really significant question is not *when* life first existed on the planet, but *how* it came to be. The extreme hypotheses of those who will not admit God is the Creator defy comprehension! Francis Crick, who shared a Nobel Prize for his part in the discovery of the structure of the DNA molecule,[3] advocated the theory of Panspermia, which states that the seeds of life have been diffused throughout the universe via meteors.[4] He did not think the age of the earth was anywhere near long enough to allow for evolution.

Another extreme hypothesis is that of parallel universes. We don't have to answer questions of origin and destiny, it is maintained, since we cannot be the highest "civilization" in a framework of multiple universes.[5] And really, think about it. Parallel universes? Well, beam me up, and count me out (of this conversation)! And some people call Christians superstitious and unscientific!

> [14]And God said, "Let there be lights in the expanse of the sky to separate the day from the night, and let them serve as signs to mark seasons and days and years, [15]and let them be lights in the expanse of the sky to give light on the earth." And it was so. [16]God made two great lights—the greater light to govern the day and the lesser light to govern the night. He also made the stars. [17]God set them in the expanse of the sky to give light on the earth, [18]to govern the day and the night, and to separate light from darkness. And God saw that it was good. [19]And there was evening, and there was morning—the fourth day.

On the fourth day God makes the sun, moon and stars. It seems the lights are intentionally not called "sun" and "moon" for theological reasons: shemesh (sun) and sin (moon) are names of pagan gods! Notice that they serve us humans. "Seasons, days, years"—God is telling the story from man's perspective and with a view to his plan to bless man. Man is not the product of a blind force that did not have him in mind! We are the children of an all-wise and loving Creator.

It is objected, "But God made light before he made the sun? That doesn't make sense." Some creationists respond that he may have created the sunbeams before he made the sun itself. This does seem to be stretching it![6] The point of the writer is that God made sun, moon, and stars for man's benefit—for calendric[7] and navigational purposes.[8]

> [20]And God said, "Let the water teem with living creatures, and let birds fly above the earth across the expanse of the sky." [21]So God created the great creatures of the sea and every living and moving thing with which the water teems, according to their

> *kinds, and every winged bird according to its kind. And God saw that it was good. [22]God blessed them and said, "Be fruitful and increase in number and fill the water in the seas, and let the birds increase on the earth." [23]And there was evening, and there was morning—the fifth day.*

On the fifth day God creates birds and fish. They will inhabit the realms created on the second day (water and sky).[9]

> [24]*And God said, "Let the land produce living creatures according to their kinds: livestock, creatures that move along the ground, and wild animals, each according to its kind." And it was so. [25]God made the wild animals according to their kinds, the livestock according to their kinds, and all the creatures that move along the ground according to their kinds. And God saw that it was good.*

The sixth day sees the creation of land creatures. Notice that there is no mention of amphibians or reptiles— only mammals. That is because we are looking at the creation of land animals from the perspective of animal husbandry! The story is being told in a way meaningful to the ancient Hebrews.

> [26]*Then God said, "Let us make man in our image, in our likeness, and let them rule over the fish of the sea and the birds of the air, over the livestock, over all the earth, and over all the creatures that move along the ground."*

> [27]*So God created man in his own image, in the image of God he created him; male and female he created them.*

We have finally come to the apex of God's creative activity: the creation of man. Several surprises emerge here, both for the person who does not know God, as well as for the original readers (or hearers) of Genesis:

- Mankind is the climax of creation. We *are* special. This brings with it a tremendous responsibility—to exercise dominion or responsible lordship over the rest of nature. Whether or not intelligent life is ever found in outer space, the Bible reveals man's special and unique position in the cosmos.

- Man is created in the (spiritual) likeness of God. Though part of nature, he is separate from and above nature—because God is above nature, and we are all his children (in the broadest sense of his paternity: Acts 17:28).[10] We are not God, only an image.[11] This flies in the face of Eastern religions and New Age teaching, which heavily stresses our divine potential. The Bible does not teach *pantheism* (everything is God); nor are bodies and spirits recycled in the "circle of life." (Sorry, Simba!)
- 1:26-27 would have been sensational for the recently liberated Israelites. Pharaoh claimed to be "the image of God," but God's word informs us that we are all images of God! Everyone has heard of the boy Pharaoh, "King Tut." His full name, *Tutankhamun,* means "living image of Amon" (a god widely worshiped in Egypt). The image of God is not the exclusive right of royalty, for we are all God's image.
- Male and female constitute mankind; male is incomplete without female,[12] to the delight of feminists and to the chagrin of misogynist male chauvinists. Not only that, both male and female are included in "the image of God."[13]

> [28]*God blessed them and said to them, "Be fruitful and increase in number; fill the earth and subdue it. Rule over the fish of the sea and the birds of the air and over every living creature that moves on the ground."*
>
> [29]*Then God said, "I give you every seed-bearing plant on the face of the whole earth and every tree that has fruit with seed in it. They will be yours for food.* [30]*And to all the beasts of the earth and all the birds of the air and all the creatures that move on the ground—everything that has the breath of life in it—I give every green plant for food." And it was so.*

After creating (later on in the sixth day) man, his most noble creature,[14] God gives him a commission: to be fruitful and multiply! This has been called the one command all mankind has always obeyed! And there is ample reason to believe that this command was obeyed swiftly, even before the Fall of man.[15]

Moving from the biological to the theological, as disciples, we too have a commission to be fruitful and fill the earth: to bear fruit for Jesus Christ and fill the earth with the knowledge of the Lord. The "Great Commission" (Matthew 28:19-20) applies to all Christians; there are no exceptions. Disciples are called to reproduce "after their kind": disciples making disciples who in turn will make more disciples, and so on.

Yes, man is neither an insignificant insect nor a cog in the great universal machine, but the crown of creation. And God has a great purpose for his children (to know him), as well as a mission (to populate the earth with spiritual children).

> [31]*God saw all that he had made, and it was very good. And there was evening, and there was morning—the sixth day.*

Everything God created was good. And not just good, but *very* good. At first there was nothing wrong with the physical creation. Everything God created was well-designed. No engineer, no craftsman, no artist has ever produced a design superior to those the LORD made and implemented in the creation.

Good, very good! This is the LORD's assessment of his own work. But if God created only good things, where did evil come from?

Conclusion

In Genesis 1:6-31 God reveals his impressive work of creation, the fact that it is good and that we have a responsibility to keep it that way. He also shows us something of his heart: We see clearly his foresight, forethought and yearning for spiritual children. Having offspring is a calculated risk, for when free will is present, the outcome cannot be guaranteed. Parents all long for their children to grow up, dare great things and successfully make an impact on this world. How much more can this be said of the Lord Almighty? Indeed, God dared to create!

Theological Question: Did God Create Evil?

"If God created everything that exists, and evil exists, God must have created evil. How do you explain that?" So runs the often asked question about the goodness of God.[16]

To answer it we must first know something about free will, and then something about opposites. God created the material world, yes, as well as the spiritual world. The spiritual world includes beings with free will. Free-willed beings chose to rebel against God; Christians understand that at this point sin entered the cosmos. Evil did not exist before that time.

Second, let's examine opposites. Cold is the opposite of hot. Large is the opposite of small. Evil is the opposite of good. These are all opposites by definition. We say God created the earth, people, atoms and light. We do not normally say God created large and small, cold and hot.[17] "Small" exists because "large" exists. In the same way, cold and hot are relative.

God is good and the opposite of God (good) is evil. Until beings, heavenly and earthly, actively rebelled or willfully used their free will to defy God's sovereignty, evil existed only in principle. Practically speaking, it did not exist. Briefly put, until there was rebellion against God (*opposition* of his good and perfect will), there was no evil (the *opposite* of good) in the world.

Therefore, the answer to the question is surprising. The existence of evil is really a stumbling block only for those who do not want to believe, who find subordinating their lives to God inconvenient and undesirable.

Notes

1. In fact the New Revised Stardard Version (NRSV) translates the word in 1:6 as "dome."

2. For what it's worth, gymnosperms precede angiosperms, which is what the fossil record confirms. However, plant life precedes life in the oceans, which, if it is meant to be taken as a statement of biology, is at odds with the fossil evidence.

Incidentally, the oft cited Miller-Urey experiment of the 1950s, in which a few amino acids (part of the DNA molecule) were synthesized in an apparatus simulating the "primordial sea," gives no comfort to the atheistic evolutionist, since (a) the assumptions made about the primeval (reducing) atmosphere have now been abandoned in favor of an oxidizing atmosphere with different initial gases, (b) this experiment *never* produced life, nor even DNA, which is tens of thousands of times more complex than an amino acid, and (c) even if the findings validated abiogenesis (the origination of living organisms from lifeless matter) (which they most emphatically did *not*) all they would prove is that God could have synthesized life in the sea. No proof would have relieved us of the necessity of God in the process.

3. Watson and Crick discovered that Deoxyribonucleic acid (DNA) has a double-helical structure. In my view DNA is God's personal signature on all his masterpieces of life, since it contains the coded information for the structure and physiology of every life form. I wonder whether Darwin would have dared to hazard his theory if he had understood the sheer complexity of genetics and reproduction—thousands of times more complex than he had imagined! Yet the more complex, the greater the faith it requires to ascribe it to pure chance, and the greater the glory which we are forced to give to God!

4. Interestingly (though inconclusively), in the summer of 1996, the Antarctic 1984 Martian Meteorite was analyzed and determined to possibly contain fossil remains of microorganisms. For a level-headed assessment of the find, see W. Wayt Gibbs and Corey S. Powell, "Bugs in the Data: The controversy over Martian life is just beginning" in *Scientific American*, 20-22, October 1996. Incidentally, whether or not life exists or has existed elsewhere in the universe is no theological problem for Christians, since the Bible nowhere teaches *for* or *against* the possibility.

5. We don't have time (even in a footnote) to address the complexity of quantum physics and astrophysics, but one thing is certain and predicted according to physics: It would be impossible to empirically verify the existence of "parallel universes," since there can be no point of contact between them and our own! Thus the advocate of multiple universes is conveniently excused from the (impossible) task of scientifically justifying his position. At its frontier, modern physics is increasingly becoming *metaphysics!*

6. Yes, I know that, as Einstein predicted, light can bend or "stretch." Enough frivolity. Let us return to the text; you're probably spending too much time reading footnotes.

7. For example, see Psalm 104:19.

8. If we take day four as a statement of science, it may be legitimate to argue that the word here for "made" (1:16) isn't the usual word Hebrew for

create, *bara'*, but the word *'asah*, meaning "to shape or form." This being the case, the sun and moon had already existed, but their light couldn't reach the earth because of the thick cloud cover. Some scholars hold that the sun, moon and stars weren't useful to man for purposes of measurement as long as the "vapor canopy" (alleged to have existed on the basis of Genesis 2:6) shrouded the earth, which disappeared completely in the flood of Noah. All this seems highly dubious, however. As we've seen, *bara'* can be used in different senses, and it's far from certain that the change in verb is scientifically determined.

9. Notice that he does this *before* making the land animals. Scientists today believe that birds developed *from* reptiles. Obviously, if we take Genesis 1 as a statement of literal scientific fact, the literalists have a problem.

10. The Hebrew preposition b^e (in) seems to be synonymous with k^e, meaning "as," in Genesis 5:3. God is making man *as* his image. See also Exodus 6:3, where God appears "b^e God Almighty." Hence Paul (oddly, from the perspective of most English translations) can say man "*is* the image...of God" in 1 Corinthians 11:7.

11. In the words of Henri Blocher, professor of systematic theology at the Faculté Libre de Théologie Evangélique, Vaux-sur-Seine, France, "Mankind remains infinitely lower than his Creator; he is mere creature and nothing more...the Bible excludes the pagan theme of the divination of man and all the dreams of hidden divinity and self-creation. It does not follow the Babylonian mythology with its humanity molded with divine blood [the blood of the god Kingu]. The spirit conferred on mankind does not emanate from it as if it were a portion of the Spirit of God." *In the Beginning* (Downers Grove: InterVarsity Press, 1984, trans. by David G. Preston), 82.

12. It has been suggested 1:27 should be rendered (emphasis added) "*although* male and female," meaning that the image of God does not have male and female components, but that God created male and female beings in his image, even though he himself is male. This view, however, does not commend itself to many.

13. As Blocher (see note 11 above) insightfully puts it, "...there is a kind of subtle balance. In all earthly relationships, the man represents God more obviously than does the woman: in active transcendency, in keeping an objective distance, in leadership and in work. But we realize at once that it is the woman who best represents humanity in relationship *with God:* in the face-to-face relationship with the Lord, every human being, male or female, must accept a feminine position, existing from him and for him, receiving and bearing the seed of his word, receiving and bearing the name he gives.... Each of us, man and woman, finds it easier to live one dimension of the human portion, being as the image of God; one represents him, one corresponds to him" (*In the Beginning*, 104-105).

14. This isn't mere biological narcissism! It's the clear teaching of the Bible and the only common-sense approach to our world. The "ultra-green" (environmentalists) may blush to admit that humankind is the highest creature, as though this were somehow unfair or against egalitarianism. Yet these same people (inconsistently) refuse to attribute to animals, plants, bacteria and viruses what Christians know is unique to man: spirituality.

Once I was delivering a lecture at Stockholm University. Someone in the crowd was offended when I described man as "the apex of creation." Looking for some point of agreement, I asked whether he didn't believe we were more valuable than mosquitoes. He balked, and then, searching for a relatable example, I said: "Suppose terrorists came in and took your grandmother hostage. They also captured a mosquito. Placing their guns to the head of each, they tell you to choose which one to allow to live. Which one is more important? How would you choose?" His response stunned me: "Well, that depends on your perspective. If I were a mosquito...!"

We should be grateful that we are being called on to care for our environment and understand our place in nature. But the woolly minded perspective of the ultra-green devalues man, created in the image of God, relativizing his worth, and contradicts the teaching of God that we are to have *dominion* over nature.

15. We'll discuss the question of the matter of the offspring of Adam and Eve in Chapter 12.

16. For a thorough discussion of the matter, see C. S. Lewis' book *The Problem of Pain.*

17. These are analytic categories; they have no objective existence of their own, i.e. *other* things must first exist before they can be considered cold and hot.

4
Creation Concluded

Day Seven

In this chapter we finish off our analysis of the creation week. God has transformed *chaos* (disorder) to *cosmos* (order). The waters have been separated to allow for the formation of sky and land, followed by the creation of plant and animal life. Finally, man was created on the earth. All this took six days.[1]

> *2:1Thus the heavens and the earth were completed in all their vast array.*
>
> *2By the seventh day God had finished the work he had been doing; so on the seventh day he rested from all his work. 3And God blessed the seventh day and made it holy, because on it he rested from all the work of creating that he had done.*
>
> *4aThis is the account of the heavens and the earth when they were created.*

As the King James Version puts 2:4a (which, in this case, is a little closer to the Hebrew than the NIV), "These are the generations of the heavens and of the earth when they were created." Yes, the word "generations" is *toledoth*. The first "generation" of Genesis is the generation of the natural world.

The seventh day marks the end of the creation week. God "rests" from his work. This is a clue that Genesis was written

A Good Night's Sleep

How may we implement the wisdom of the Sabbath, applying the Old Testament principle to New Testament times?

- God designed us to sleep. It is not "spiritual" to deprive yourself for deprivation's sake! (Colossians 2:20-23). Never think you are superior to others just because you sleep fewer hours. Do you love to call attention to how little sleep you get by on?
- A 1996 poll found the average American sleeps seven hours and fifty minutes a night—except Saturday night, when he slumbers eight hours and fifty minutes! But is your goal to be average? Disciples have a reason to get up, and often after a long night we will need to rise early to pray (Mark 1:32-35; Luke 4:40-42). The Bible neither speaks of the biological need for eight hours of sleep, nor of the eight-hour workday.[2] Most disciples can accomplish more than the average person, and on less sleep. The Spirit will strengthen us (Ephesians 3:16). It is a fact that those who are truly excited about their relationship with God will be brighter, more energetic, more light-hearted than those who drag through life without a friendship with God!
- On the other hand, too little sleep will erode our alertness and compromise our judgment, and we are commanded to "be alert" (Ephesians 6:18; 1 Thessalonians 5:6; 1 Peter 5:8).
- A good rule of thumb: Sleep until you are refreshed when feasible, but never compromise your walk with God and your mission to spread the Word!

- Working every day of the week is clearly not God's plan. Working late may be necessary occasionally, but be careful you don't sacrifice your family for career. It's not worth it! (See 1 Timothy 6:6-10.)
- In our increasingly secular society, there will be pressure to sacrifice family time and "spiritual times" for economic reasons, often to maintain a higher standard of living. (Remember Solomon's words in Ecclesiastes 5:10-12.)
- While we mustn't insist on our "resting rights" (2 Corinthians 6:5, 11:27), God does purpose to give us sleep, as Psalm 127:1-2 plainly says. Be disciplined not only about getting up in the morning, but also going to bed at night.[3]
- Watch out: Naps have potential for good (Mark 4:38), but also for sloth (Proverbs 6:6-11). In our self-indulgent society, the nap is grossly overdone. In general, if we are so tired we can sleep through a storm (as Jesus did), we probably needed the nap!
- The principle of the Sabbath is indeed helpful for our time. "All work and no play makes Jack a dull boy." Everyone needs a break. God designed us not to be machines, but human beings.

in the time of the Israelites (and not necessarily earlier), since the references to the Sabbath would have meant little before the giving of the Law at Sinai.

Here in Genesis we are given no indication as to why God rested on the seventh day. We do know that it was not because God was fatigued and needed the rest as we do (Isaiah 40:28). In the light of the later Sabbath law, it would appear it was something of a precedent set purely for the benefit of his people. Clearly, it is not God's will that we be fatigued, but refreshed (see Psalm 127:1-2; Matthew 11:28-30; and 1 John 5:3-4).

Excursus: The Sabbath

Several modern groups teach that we are under obligation to keep the Sabbath. The simplest answer to those who teach Sabbath-keeping is Colossians 2:16-17. (See also Galatians 4:8-11; Hebrews 4:9; and especially Romans 14:5-6.) In fact no one in "Christendom" consistently keeps the Sabbath today, for that would entail not only the seventh day (Friday sundown to Saturday sundown), but also the Sabbatical and Jubilee Years (read Leviticus 25). With separation of church and state under the new covenant, observation of the biblical Sabbath is, quite frankly, impossible to implement.

The early church (as seen in Acts) used Sabbaths for evangelistic purposes, knowing that they would find Jews in the synagogues. The main meeting day for disciples was Sunday, not Saturday (Acts 20:7).[4]

Perspectives on the Two Creation Accounts

One may legitimately ask why there are two creation accounts. Are liberal theologians correct when they say that these are two contradictory stories? Why don't the details neatly mesh together? What can we conclude from the text?

- To begin with, the focus of Genesis is *man*, not the creation. Genesis 1 gives us a panorama, then chapter 2 zooms in on man and his relationship with God. The focus will narrow further as Genesis moves from Abraham to his descendants through Isaac and to Isaac's descendants through Jacob.
- Chapter 2 seems to have the animals being created after man, rather than before him, as in the sixth "day" of creation in chapter 1. Perhaps 2:19, which in the NIV is translated "had formed," solves the apparent problem. Most

versions translate the verb "formed," reversing the time sequence.[5] On the other hand, we are probably imposing our chronology on the text. The two accounts should be read as complementary rather than as intersecting.

• To sum up, Genesis 1 shows man's special place in the creation, while Genesis 2 shows man's special relationship with God.[6] There is no necessary contradiction.

The Second Account

The second creation account begins in the middle of the verse 4.[7]

> [4b]*When the LORD God made the earth and the heavens—[5]and no shrub of the field had yet appeared on the earth and no plant of the field had yet sprung up, for the LORD God had not sent rain on the earth and there was no man to work the ground, [6]but streams came up from the earth and watered the whole surface of the ground—[7]the LORD God formed the man from the dust of the ground and breathed into his nostrils the breath of life, and the man became a living being.*

Rather than taking 2:5 to refer to plant-life (which was created on the third "day") we should see this in an *agrarian* context. This was before the rise of agriculture, which makes its debut in Genesis 4.

Man is made from dust. Not too flattering![8] This does not contradict the truth in chapter 1 that he is made in the image of God. God has always been able to put treasure in jars of clay (see 2 Corinthians 4:7). With the creation of man comes the creation of woman, and we will say much more about this in Chapter 7.

The word translated "man" in Genesis 1 and 2 is also the word translated "Adam." In fact, *Adam* is the Hebrew word for "man."[9] There is clearly a word-play going on in these chapters. On the one hand, Adam is the first historical man, and on the other, Adam is mankind, wrapped up in one individual. Both figures tend to blend into one another, and it is not always easy to tell which the author has in mind—or whether both are intended.

God's Existence

God is introduced in the early chapters of Genesis. He, after all, is the main character in his book, the Bible. No attempt is made to prove his existence. As has been somewhat sarcastically quipped, this was written for those who know better.

We meet a preexistent sovereign God, whose power is unlimited. We see his wisdom, moral nature and his grace—a theme highly developed in Genesis. We meet a God who desired fellowship with man, then created man, and never abandoned the pursuit of his creature.

He is our Creator—not some lesser god as in the pagan religions or Gnosticism. He is good and what he makes is good. Man is the crowning accomplishment of his creative processes! And because everything God does has a reason behind it, we can trust him. Before we close this chapter, it may be helpful to consider the cause and effects of atheism.

The Problem with Atheism

- *Atheism is impossible to defend.* It is an anti-position.[10] "A-theism" [not-theism, not-"belief in God"] maintains that there is no infinite, all-knowing, all-powerful God in the universe. But how could you prove this? To prove that no all-knowing being exists in the universe you yourself would have to have infinite knowledge of the entire universe! You would have to *be* God to prove that there is no God, which is clearly nonsensical.
- Atheists are terribly outnumbered. Throughout history the overwhelming majority of human beings have believed in God, and even today the number of true atheists is rela-

tively small. Moreover, many so-called atheists are closet theists. When they make reference to "Mother Nature," or make statements like "That's not fair!", they show that they don't have any idea how to explain the universe without recourse to a higher being. And fairness is meaningless if there is no absolute standard by which to measure injustice. "Hey, he broke the rules!" someone exclaims. "What rules?" says the modern intellectual, adrift in the sea of relativity. The denial of God is the denial of absolutes.[11] Not that being in the minority means you're wrong (far from it!); it's just that you'd better have some convincing evidence if you would refute 95% of humanity! Try as hard as they will, no one can dislodge belief in God from the human race. Indeed, "God has set eternity in the hearts of men" (Ecclesiastes 3:11).

- Atheism is powerless to change the world for good. Atheism does not work. Politically, it has been shown over and over to be a failure. Socially, it is a force destructive of family life and virtue. No lives have ever been changed for the better through atheism. No world-shaking movements have revolutionized the world for good through this anti-religion. Because it is not rooted in reality, it strands us ethically, leaving us high and dry on the sands of relativism. The fruit of atheism is selfishness, insecurity, loneliness and confusion..

- Atheism will fail in the end. Today we can convince ourselves that there's no policeman out there, drive as fast as we like and scoff at the notion of authority. Atheism does appeal to selfish human nature—don't let anyone suggest otherwise. But one day we *will* see the flashing blue lights. Just because you don't get pulled over tomorrow, don't jump to the conclusion that there is no God in the universe.

Take Some Advice

As we saw in Chapter 1, Genesis introduces us to God. It is here that we shake his hand. A personal relationship with God is fabulous and is central to Christianity. Yet many of the details in our discussion of creation are definitely not central to the faith; they are peripheral. Keep your eye on the heart, not the externals; on content, not form.

The last two chapters have covered a lot of ground and suggested a number of possibilities. Maybe you are stimulated and excited about some of the new possibilities. You are coming rather quickly to some different views of God and his word. Do be gracious to those who may not share your view, and be humble!

Finally, don't jump to conclusions. Don't be dogmatic in areas you are only just beginning to explore! Be gentle with those who think differently, and prepare yourself for a serious consideration of the nature of Genesis chapter 1. There is so much more evidence to weigh.

Notes

1. The college joke about God partying six days and then "pulling an all-nighter" is wrong on two counts: first, unlike some college students, God is responsible and wastes no time; second, the Bible speaks of a six-day, not a seven-day, creation.

2. Since the Bible is silent in these areas, we need to make sure we aren't making our own rules and calling them God's.

3. For many of us, author included, the second discipline is more demanding than the first!

4. Sunday as a "day of rest" finds its way into Christianity after two centuries. Consider the testimony of two early second century writers, Ignatius and "Barnabas," writer of the spurious Epistle of Barnabas:

> If, then, those who had lived in antiquated practices came to newness of hope, no longer keeping the Sabbath but living in accordance with the Lord's Day [Sunday, kyriake, the Lord's day, in Greek], on which our life also arose through him and his death (which some deny), the mystery through which we came to believe, and because of which we patiently endure in order that we might be found to be disciples of Jesus Christ, our only teacher... (Ignatius, Magnesians 9:1).

Finally, he says to them, "I cannot bear your new moons and Sabbaths." You see what he means: "It is not the present Sabbaths that are acceptable to me, but the one that I have made; on that Sabbath, after I have set everything at rest, I will create the beginning of an eighth day, which is the beginning of another world." This is why we spend the eighth day in celebration, the day on which Jesus both arose from the dead and, after appearing again, ascended into heaven (Epistle of Barnabas, 15:8-9). From such passages it is clear that early Christians were not bound by any Sabbath observance.

5. In Hebrew the distinction between perfect and pluperfect must be determined by context, since there exists no separate form for the pluperfect (past perfect).

6. Two books concerning creation which may be helpful are Daniel Vestal's *The Doctrine of Creation,* Nashville: Convention Press, 1983 and John Clayton's *The Source,* South Bend: Clayton, 1976.

7. Remember that verse divisions were not brought into the text until the sixteenth century. What is awkward for us (breaking off in the middle of a verse) was smooth and easy for earlier readers of the Bible, before the days of verse divisions.

8. In the Qur'an, the sacred text of the Muslims, he is made from a clot of blood!

9. There is another word, *'ish,* but this word does not appear until 2:24. *Adam* is related to the word *adamah,* meaning *ground.*

10. Self-styled intellectuals constantly confuse their terms! A true atheist says there is no God—not that he doesn't believe in one. An agnostic says that [even if there were a God] God is unknowable; therefore we can neither affirm nor deny his existence. When men and women say "I don't know if there's a God," they are neither atheists nor agnostics. They are simply wishy-washy—or they have never examined the facts.

11. Extremely few intellectuals who are atheists are consistent at this point. A true atheist rejects absolute morality. The consistent philosopher of modern times was Friedrich Nietzsche (1844-1900), who taught that if there is no God ("God is dead"), then there is no true right and wrong. All morals are mere matters of opinion. Nietzsche predicted accordingly that the twentieth century would be the most meaningless and the bloodiest century in the history of the human race to date. He was right. Man staggers morally, groping for meaning. Atheistic governments have exterminated countless millions of their own citizens in this century: Russia, China, Cambodia, Germany to mention just a few scenes of horror. Ironically, Nietzsche himself died alone and insane.

5
How Long Is a Day?

The Six Creation Days

In this chapter we tackle the issue of the creation days: whether they are literal days, or ages, or something totally different. Some of the material in this chapter is admittedly a little technical. Don't read it too quickly; give it some time, and the reward will be well worth the effort. To begin with, let's address the question of the age of the earth.

A Young Earth?

You may have noticed that there is no date in Genesis 1:1, no footnote telling us the exact year of Creation. What about the date 4004 B.C., often taught in Sunday School curricula? This was the guess of the Irish Archbishop Ussher (1581-1656), Professor of Theological Controversies at Trinity College Dublin. By adding genealogies together, he arrived at October 23, 4004 B.C. as the date of Creation and 2349 B.C. as the time of Noah's Flood. But there are some serious problems with this approach.

1. As we'll soon see in our commentary on Genesis 5, we simply cannot add genealogies together and arrive at solid dates, since they often skip generations.
2. Even if this methodology were sound, it still isn't possible to date Genesis 1:1, since it precedes the first creation "day."

3. There are plenty of written records from Egypt and Mesopotamia from well before 3000 B.C., so Ussher's flood date hardly fits with the facts. For example, the great pyramids of Egypt are some 4500 years old!

Though Ussher's view has been discredited, there are still a number of Bible believers who remain convinced that the earth cannot be more than a few thousand years old. One movement committed to a young age for the earth, and which rejects all attempts to vindicate the currently accepted age of around 15 billion years for the universe and 4 billion years for the earth, is "Scientific Creationism." In the view of most scientists it is unscientific, nothing more than an exotic and rather forced interpretation of the Creation and Flood accounts to accommodate preconceived religious notions.

Are the creationists right? Is the earth only a few thousand years old? Are all scientists fundamentally in error as to their conclusions about the fossils and the age of the universe? If they are right, why does our world give every appearance of being ancient?

Navel Gazing

Sometimes it is argued that God created the earth with an appearance of age. The "Omphalos Theory," popularized by Gosse in 1857, is named after the Greek word for "navel," *omphalos*. Since (it is claimed) Adam was formed as a fully adult male, presumably he had a belly button. He may have appeared to be 25 or 30 years old, but in fact he was only seconds old. The trees of Eden, by the same token, would have shown tree rings (annual growth rings). Simply put, God made the earth with an built-in appearance of age.

But there is a problem here. Scientific evidence cannot be claimed for both a young earth and an ancient appearance. There should be no shred of evidence for a "young earth" if the Omphalos Theory is correct![1] You just cannot have it both ways. Yet creationists often put forward the Omphalos Theory among their many arguments.

Those who take Genesis 1 literally criticize radiometric dating, a reliable technique that yields great ages for the earth.[2] They often forget that even before Darwin (his *Origin of Species* was written in 1859), most geologists and churchmen alike believed in an ancient earth, based on the fossil evidence and the geologic column. There are many methods one can use to show that the earth is far older than a few thousand years, and the interested reader can pursue this in further study.[3]

Some Bible believers insist on a complete instantaneous creation. But must it really be instantaneous? Is it less miraculous if it comes in stages? God's usual way is actually to work through *processes,* not instantaneous fiat (commanded) creation. God gives us children, yet still there is a nine-month waiting period. And, like it or not, character change comes about slowly (Romans 5:3-4). How would endurance exist otherwise? (Can you imagine God saying, "No need to diet—just fast for two hours and you'll lose all your excess weight," or "Hang on now, if you persevere for four seconds you'll be a totally transformed, dynamic individual"?) Creation is no less creation just because it occurs over a period of time![4]

So when *was* the earth made? God has already said when: "In the beginning." If we are wise, we won't get too much more specific than that. The earth might be young, and it might be old, but neither possibility is clinched by the Bible.[5]

"Scientific" Creationism?

Some Bible believers adhere to an interpretation of Genesis which they call "Scientific Creationism."[6] By this they usually mean that the earth was created in six literal 24-hour periods some six thousand years ago. Furthermore, they insist that, since this is the case, all "prehistoric" life forms—such as the dinosaurs—were drowned in the Genesis Flood,[7] which is also responsible for the major geological features on the planet—even the Grand Canyon and the Himalayan Mountains.[8]

Why take time to highlight this group? Because they have shaped the thinking of many churchgoers, particularly in the United States, and we must look carefully to see if their conclusions are really justified or if they are required of those who believe in the authority of Scripture.

The creationist strategy is usually threefold:

1. They attempt to show the biases of various scientists and how they disagree with one another. In their view modern scientists are not to be trusted because of their rejection of Scripture; only creationist scientists understand the truth about the genesis of the cosmos and life on earth. All others are sometimes linked in some sort of conspiracy to suppress the truth.

2. To proclaim that the earth is only a few thousand years old and "prove" this by casting doubts on the accuracy of established scientific dating techniques.[9] All forms of evolutionary science are viewed with the utmost distaste and suspicion. The earth is much too young, it is held, to have allowed evolution to occur.[10]

3. To object to microevolution (small changes at the specific level) on the grounds of the problems of macroevolution (the Theory of Evolution itself). For example, deriding the evolution of dogs and wolves from a common ancestor (i.e., they must have been created independently)[11] because there is no proof that a reptile could transmute into a mammal (a macromutation).

While their goal of defending the reliability of Scripture is a noble one, this methodology is not without its problems. We cannot argue with the fact that there is a conspiracy to "suppress the truth" but it is not just among scientists. The whole world is guilty of this one—and the Bible says as much (Romans 1:18). The conspiracy is not against "scientific truth" as such, but the truth about religion, morality, sexuality and ethics.

Many scientists are Bible believers, and many are not, but extremely few adhere to the conclusions and antics of the "scientific creationists." Of course there is bias among scientists, although they are supposed to be objective in their fields of expertise. But there is also great bias among theologians. Showing how two evolutionists disagree no more "disproves" evolution than showing how two theologians disagree "disproves" God.

As for dating techniques, the great antiquity of the earth was well established—even among churchmen—nearly a century before Darwin. All dating methods yield great ages for the earth. Arguments creationists use for the "refutation" of dating techniques which consistently yield a great age for the earth, the solar system and the entire universe, are ludicrous to the point of embarrassment.[12]

Finally, the matter of macroevolution. Evolution is defined properly as "development." Life has developed on the earth, and this fact no one disputes. The question is one of extent. Does evolution entail only small changes at the specific level (microevolution), which everyone seems to accept, or does it entail macroevolutionary changes, such as the development of amphibians from fish, which is far more difficult to demonstrate? Actually many of the creationists' insights are valid, but their conclusions are too radical; they throw out the baby (the amazing adaptability God programmed into life) with the bath water (the totality of arguments both good and bad relied upon by scientists in various fields).

Many men and women seeking an intelligent faith have been turned away from the Bible by creationism. Once again, it must be stated that creationism is not the same thing as Creation. You can hold to the second without advocating the first. Creationism is only one of dozens of interpretations of Genesis; Creation is the fact referred to in the text of Genesis and by virtue of which we live and breathe today.

Literal Days?

What is meant by the word "literal"? What does it mean when Christians say they take the Bible "literally"? Before we proceed any further in our discussion of the days, we need to clarify what we mean by "literal" and "literally." Although literalism can mean interpreting words in their natural sense, it has another meaning as well: taking metaphors and symbols as though they were not metaphorical or symbolic. For this reason I prefer not to say that I take the Bible "literally." I prefer to say I take the Bible "at face value."

Certainly the prose sections of the Bible are to be taken literally—apart, of course, from figures of speech. Yet, the Bible has many poetic sections which cannot and aren't meant to be taken literally. For example, Psalm 91:4 speaks of God's wings and feathers. Yet, I've met no one who takes this literally. In the same way, sections of the Bible, like the book of Revelation, which is full of figurative speech and symbolism, cannot *possibly* be taken "literally." With this in mind, a better way to describe our approach to the scriptures is to say that we take them "at face value" or "seriously." Nearly always, context shows us whether a passage is meant literally or figuratively.

Well, are the days of Genesis 1 literal days? Interestingly, among Christian thinkers and writers through the centuries, the literal interpretation has not been the dominant one. Many, many Bible believers have taken the "days" in a different sense. (Their various approaches will be detailed below.)

A more literal translation of Genesis 2:4 would be, "This is the account of the heavens and the earth *in the day* ["when," NIV] God created them." The Hebrew *bᵉyom* literally means "in the day," not "when," although strictly speaking, the NIV translation is accurate. The point is that in 2:4 the word "day" is used in a nonliteral sense, actually summing up six days!

In the Bible "day" can refer to a twenty-four-hour period, or the daylight portion of that same period, or it is even compared to "a thousand years"! On top of all this, "evening and morning" are attributes of the first three days, even before the sun is made (or made visible). Are we *sure* these are literal days?

The ancients did not always think of time in the way we moderns do. They thought more in terms of quality (the kind of day), whereas we think more in terms of quantity (twenty-four hours). We understand the principle because we use "days" in the qualitative (as opposed to quantitative) sense, when we speak of "glory days," or when we say things like, "In my day, a Big Mac cost a quarter." It would be inappropriate to ask "Exactly which day are you talking about?" or "How many glory days were there?"

Then it might be asked whether God literally rested (Genesis 2:2). Psalm 121 seems to state clearly that God never rests. If the rest isn't literal, why does the day on which God "rested" have to be a literal day?

Next, Day Seven is *unclosed.* Perhaps you noticed that the six creation days all close with the same formula: "And there was evening, and there was morning—the -*nth* day." In fact, Hebrews 4 insists that there remains a Sabbath rest for God's people because the day is still open. It was never closed out! Jesus' reasoning in John 5:17, in stating that God is "always at work to this very day," presumes that God is working *on the Sabbath.* This is yet another instance where "day" cannot possibly be construed literally.

A strong argument against literalism is seen when we consider what it means if the sixth day is a literal day. After all the animals were made, Adam was created. Do you have any idea how busy Adam's first "day" would have been? First, he is created and receives commands from God (2:15-17). Then he is apparently lonely (2:18). Then he names the animals (except the fish). 2:19 says he named *all* the beasts of the field and birds of the air. How long would it take to name millions of species? Even at the rate of one per second, Adam wouldn't have even had time to name 75,000 animals! Then he's put into a deep sleep for the operation (2:21). After Eve has been formed, she and Adam meet, he recites his poem for her (2:23), then they become man and wife. (What did you accomplish on *your* wedding day?) Literalism actually demands the above (absurd) interpretation.

The evidence against the days of creation being literal days is substantial. So what are the alternatives?

Five Major Approaches

There are five major approaches to Genesis 1. It must be noted that, with respect to all the major interpretations we are considering, each is taught by a number of persons who believe in the Bible and hold the Genesis account to be true.

1. *The Literal Theory.* God created everything in six literal 24-hour days. The Literal Theory may be the simplest interpretation of the passage, and the view is often taught to our children in Sunday School, yet we have given several reasons against this interpretation.

2. *The Gap Theory.* In the "gap" between Genesis 1:1 and 1:2 a universal cataclysm took place. In this ingenious hypothesis, the original creation was destroyed and God started over. For example, the dinosaurs were exterminated, their fossils left in the ground.[13] This view posits that the six days are the time of God's *re-creation* of the earth. The theory is based on a possible but unusual translation of the Hebrew verb *hay^{e}tah* ("was") in 1:1. *Hay^{e}tah* can (rarely) be rendered "became," which is the justification for the Gap Theory.[14] This theory, suggested by some patristic and medieval writers, would probably never have become popular—especially in the nineteenth century—were it not for the tension churchmen felt between

Genesis 1 (taken literally) and the discoveries of science in the previous century or so, especially in the fossil realm.

3. *Revelatory Day Theory.* How did the Genesis writer know what happened at Creation? The Revelatory Day Theory suggests God revealed what happened in stages. On seven successive days Moses received revelation, each day "seeing" God's work in different aspects of his creation. This theory attempts to allow more time between the days, to overcome the uncomfortable nature (for some) of the "creation week." This is another nineteenth century stab at reconciling Genesis with the plain antiquity of the earth, and it has few adherents.

4. *Day-Age Theory:* A very popular view among Bible believers, in the Day-Age Theory: Each "day" is a geologic age.[15] Like the previous view, this allows for the ancient earth evidenced by science. This Theory seems to concede too much, while lacking any biblical support. It would never have been devised had the conflict between Darwinians and churchmen not happened. Some Day-Age proponents believe each age lasts 1000 years.[16]

5. *Literary Theory:* The days are not meant to be taken literally. Rather, they are a literary device for communicating the truth about the creation. The original readers of Genesis, sharing the author's culture, understood exactly what he meant. The scheme is *logical*, not *chronological*. More needs to be said about this final possibility.

The Literary Theory
Recognizes Providence

The Literary Theory recognizes a definite structure to the creation account, a definite schema.[17] Consider how God's providence and forethought are portrayed, as each of the first three days corresponds to the following three:

Day One
God creates light.

Day Four
God creates the
light-bearers,
for man's benefit.

Day Two
God arranges the
waters and sky.

Day Five
God creates water creatures
and birds that fly in the sky.

Day Three
God makes the dry
land and vegetation.

Day Six
God creates creatures that move
on dry land and eat vegetation.
Then he creates man.

Day Seven
Rest.

Not Bound as to God's Method of Creation

The days are a framework for the truth God is communicating to his people. The literary view doesn't claim God *couldn't* have created everything in six days, or in one second, or many eons! That's because this view is not tied to any particular assumptions about biology or the age of the earth. The Genesis writer isn't presenting a strict cosmological or biological sequence, but is showing how God prepared the world for human habitation. The literary view speaks clearly, regardless of the shifting sands of scientific opinion, for it stands above them.

Carefully Constructed

Genesis never purports to be a scientific account of "what happened."[18] It is a carefully constructed account, however, based on the calculated use of symbolic numbers, especially 3, 10 and 7. Many biblical scholars have studied the text of Genesis as a whole, and chapter 1 in particular, and have discovered what may be a masterful inner structure.[19]

Recognizes the Historical Situation

This view recognizes Genesis 1 (and in fact the whole of Genesis) as a stinging condemnation of rival stories circulating in Egypt, Palestine, Mesopotamia and the rest of the Mediterranean world at the time. The seven-day schema stands in stark contrast to (and in judgment of) contemporary Near Eastern creation accounts, in which man is little more than an afterthought, as well as a source of irritation to the gods.[20]

Nature of God

The literary view shows that God is a God of order (1 Corinthians 14:33). It also teaches that the universe is not the result of chance, but of careful planning. As we have seen, there is a specific historical and literary context to the book of Genesis as a whole.

Sabbath Doctrine

The literary view recognizes that Genesis 1 provides a theology of the Sabbath, which would have been highly relevant to the ancient Israelites, who had just come into a covenant relationship with God.

Richness of the Account

In attempting to interpret Genesis 1 (and 2) "scientifically," many men and women miss the richness of the descriptions, symbolism, numerology, poetry and careful construction of the account. Of the five major theories, the literary view best illuminates the features set out above—which tend to be minimized by the other approaches to the Creation account. In the words of Vestal:

> ...Genesis 1-2 is historical narrative in pictorial form. It abbreviates a long history and immense periods of time in language that translates history as well as transcends it. We are not dealing with myth or legend, which presents

an idea in the form of a story. Nature is not personified or dramatized as in nonbiblical accounts. And from other parts of Scripture, both Old and New Testaments, we know that Genesis describes actual events and persons. But neither are we dealing with a strict or scientific narrative that would have no meaning whatsoever to the early Israelites. Rather, we are dealing with a majestic piece of literature, divinely inspired and directed, that is both truth and beauty. Its linguistic and artistic arrangement is profound, and it must be interpreted in light of that arrangement.[21]

Which View Is Right?

You will have to weigh the evidence and make your own decision about which view is right. Contemporary religious and archeological evidence (see Appendix C) weighs more heavily in favor of the literary view than any of the other possibilities, yet the theological and scientific evidence is still in the process of being sifted by God-fearing men and women who accept the Bible as the word of God.[22] On the question of the nature of the "days" there is certainly some latitude for differences of opinion—just as many topics in Genesis and the rest of Scripture are capable of bearing more than one interpretation.

Whichever view persuades you, remember this: Don't go looking for verses which might support your leaning, bending them (and the facts) to the teaching of your denomination. Begin rather with the verses (and good science); then determine your position. Finally, in all things let us demonstrate charity toward those with whom we may differ. The precise nature of the six days of creation is far from being an issue of salvation. And doesn't Romans 14:1 tell us not to pass judgment (on others) when it comes to disputable matters?

So how long is a day? That depends!

Notes

1. Moreover, this approach makes God a party to deceit, since through the physical world he is misleading us. And yet the scriptures affirm over and over that God reveals truth through the creation! (Psalm 19:1; Romans 1:20).

2. While radiometric techniques occasionally yield incorrect ages (there is a built-in allowance for error, depending on the sort of radioactive decay taking place), it is unlikely an object dated at 100 million years, for example, would actually be only 10 thousand years old (the maximum age some assign to the earth). Perhaps radiometric methods give calculations 100% greater than the true age of a dinosaur bone—fair enough. But results off by 10,000%?

3. I would recommend Alan Hayward's *Creation and Evolution*, Triangle Books: London, 1985.

4. It is often alleged that the Hebrew word *bara'*, meaning "create," implies instantaneous creation. Yet Isaiah 43:1, 15 says that God "created" (*bara'*) Israel, although it took centuries (read the OT!). Even Eve, who was "created" (Genesis 1:27), came to exist through a two-stage process, the second of which involved a surgical procedure performed on her husband. Enough of this silliness!

5. In my opinion the earth is of considerable age, and I provisionally accept the current 4.3 billion year age. At any rate, no theological doctrine hinges on the age of the earth!

6. After reading 150 tracts, pamphlets and books published under the Creationist umbrella I wrote to the leading thinker of the movement, asking him to answer some of my (further) questions. To his credit, he did reply; to my disappointment, he only sent me more tracts reiterating the same lines of reasoning already adduced!

7. For a discussion of dinosaurs and the Bible, see Appendix B.

8. The title of one of the scientific creationist books (John Whitcomb is the author).

9. Especially radiometric dating, which measures the ratio of radioactive isotopes to non-radioactive isotopes, then extrapolates to a point in the past based on known decay rates. Potassium-Argon dating ($K^{40} \rightarrow Ar^{40}$) is just one of the several methods that has come under attack. For more on this subject, see Sheridan Bowman's *Radiocarbon Dating*, London: British Museum, 1990.

10. For a light discussion of Evolution, see Appendix D.

11. Not all "creationists" would list *canis lupus* as a separate species, though taxonomically speaking they are.

12. It is beyond the scope of this book to critique the creationist arguments. Suffice it to say that they are vulnerable to criticism on methodological grounds alone.

13. Isaiah 45:18 is construed to support this theory: "...[The Lord] did not create [the earth] to be empty, but formed it to be inhabited..." If the earth was not *originally* empty (in this view) then it must have *become* empty, through some global cataclysm.

14. The translation required by the Gap Theory is possible, but hard to justify. Furthermore, there is no biblical verse stating that the fall of Satan ruined the original cosmos, as adherents of this view believe. The physical decay of the cosmos is always linked with the Fall of man, not of Satan and his demons.

15. The points of agreement between Genesis 1 and modern geology are as follows: (a) The ancient earth became increasingly ordered; (b) the conditions for life, such as the formation of land and water reserves in the atmosphere as well as the sea, preceded the existence of life; (c) vegetable life preceded ani-

mal life—though this is questionable; (d) simpler forms precede more complex forms; and (e) man appears as the highest product of the creative process.

16. Based on an over-literal interpretation of Psalm 90:4. But Psalm 90 does not say 1000 years *are* a day, but that they're *like* a day. Moses (author of Psalm 90) adds "or like a watch [4 hours was a *Jewish* watch] in the night." Why not claim that 1 day = 6,000 years (24 hours ÷ 4 hours x 1000 years)? This surely isn't what Moses had in mind! By the way, whereas Psalm 90 emphasizes the *swiftness* of time (from God's perspective), 2 Peter 3 emphasizes its *slowness* (from our perspective).

17. For a clear presentation of the literary view, see John Willis, *Genesis* (commentary) Abilene: Sweet. For a helpful book that makes for lighter reading see Ernest Lucas, *Genesis Today,* London: Scripture Union, 1992.

18. For another (poetic) version of the Creation, see Proverbs 8:22-31.

19. As many Old Testament scholars have noted, many words and phrases appear a theologically planned number of times. The chance that this is coincidence is most unlikely.

- "God said" occurs 10 times: 3 times in reference to man and 7 times for all other creatures.
- The verb "to be" ("let there be") occurs 3 times for creatures in the heavens, and 7 different times for the world below.
- The verb "to make" occurs 10 times, and so does "according to their kinds."
- There are 3 blessings.
- The verb "to create" is used on 3 occasions, 3 times on the 3rd occasion.
- "And it was so" occurs 7 times.
- "And God saw that it was good" occurs 7 times.
- God either names or blesses 7 times.
- The preceding 3 heptads are independent of the structure of the 7 days!
- Genesis 1:1 has 7 words, 1:2 has 2x7 words, and 2:1-3 (which is the 7th paragraph) has 5x7 words.
- The word "earth" occurs 3x7 times, and "God" (*Elohim*) 5x7 times.
- The names of God occur 70 (7x10) times in Genesis 1-4, and prove the unity of the passage. 1x10 times it is *Yahweh* (God's personal name; see Exodus 6:3), 2x10 times *Yahweh Elohim* ("the Lord God"), and 4x10 times *Elohim* ("God").

20. Sumerian, Babylonian, Assyrian, Egyptian. For more on these creation stories, see Appendix C.

21. Daniel Vestal, *The Doctrine of Creation* (Nashville: Convention Press, 1983) pp. 33-34.

22. I myself was a proponent of the Day-Age Theory for many years, but have favored the literary view since 1984.

6

The Secret Garden

Eden

After completing his daring work of creating, God places his ultimate creation, man, in a secret garden: The Garden of Eden:[1] What was it really like to be in "paradise"? Does Eden give us any clues about what the LORD has in store for us in the next world?[2] Will the same "magic" be hovering about? How exciting it would be for an Indiana-Jones-type archeologist to discover the Garden one day! (Never mind that if we are searching for a physical garden, the Genesis account implies it might have been destroyed in the Flood![3])

We resume the narrative just after the beginning of Genesis 2:

> *2:4This is the account of the heavens and the earth when they were created.*
>
> *When the LORD God made the earth and the heavens—5and no shrub of the field had yet appeared on the earth and no plant of the field had yet sprung up, for the LORD God had not sent rain on the earth and there was no man to work the ground,6 but streams came up from the earth and watered the whole surface of the ground—7the LORD God formed the man from the dust of the ground and breathed into his nostrils the breath of life, and the man became a living being.*
>
> *8Now the LORD God had planted a garden in the east, in Eden; and there he put the man he had formed.*

We have come to the "second" creation account, which is really the second part of the Genesis account. The Bible says the Garden was located "in the east." Of course "east" is relative: east with respect to what? Almost certainly in respect to Israel. If so, this suggests Genesis was written in the time of Moses, for the benefit of the covenant people of God.

Where Is Eden?

Two places have been suggested for Eden: one in Turkey, the other in Iraq. The Turkish location lies more north than east of Israel,[4] while the Iraqi location is due east. The rivers mentioned in 2:10 (only the Tigris and the Euphrates are identifiable today) allow us to pinpoint Eden. Between these two rivers lies *Mesopotamia*.[5] The Tigris and the Euphrates are never more than 100 miles apart, running in the same direction and framing the "Fertile Crescent," or the "Cradle of Civilization" as it has been called, in which lay the ancient kingdoms of Sumer, Babylon and Assyria.[6]

Since the Tigris and Euphrates flow eastward from Turkey and empty into the Persian Gulf, it seems more likely that Eden was in the western of the two suggested locations. Several cities

have been excavated in this part of Turkey, dating to 8000 B.C.[7]
Pending further evidence, then, I favor the Turkish location.[8]

It seems the Genesis writer, despite the symbolic features
in his account,[9] nevertheless portrays Eden as a geographical
location somewhere in western Asia. Adam and Eve were
Middle Eastern, not Caucasian, but Asian,[10] with almost certainly darker skin pigmentation than portrayed in most Sunday School curricula.

Of Vegetation and Vegetables

The account says that no "shrub of the field" or "plant of
the field" had appeared before God made man. Rather than
taking this to refer to plant life in general (which was created on the third "day"), we should understand the writer
to be referring to agriculture. This was before the rise of
agriculture. After the creation of man, there are numerous
references to agriculture: 2:15, 3:17, 4:3, 4:12, 5:29, 8:22,
9:20.[11]

In the Eden narrative God is depicted as Potter (2:7, 19),
Gardener (2:8), Surgeon (2:21), and Landowner (3:8), occu-
pations to which the first readers of Genesis would have been
able to relate. God comes down to our level to communicate
with us!

Yes, God designed man to be vegetarian at first (1:29-30),
though after the Flood this was to completely change (Genesis 9:3). I myself enjoy a vegetarian dinner a couple of times
a week,[12] and there is certainly much to be said for eating
right and taking in plenty of "fruit and veggies"; however, we
must also remember that the Lord declared all foods to be
clean (Mark 7:19).

> [9]And the LORD God made all kinds of trees grow out of the ground—
> trees that were pleasing to the eye and good for food. In the middle
> of the garden were the tree of life and the tree of the knowledge of
> good and evil.

Twin Trees

There are two major trees in Eden: the Tree of Life and the Tree of the Knowledge of Good and Evil. The first tree conferred immortality (3:22). This fact shows that man is not unconditionally immortal. That is, as long as the first couple continued to eat from the tree, their lives were extended; but if they were cut off from this "Fountain of Youth," they would eventually die.

The great news is that, for Christians, the gift of God is *eternal life* in Christ Jesus (Romans 6:23; 2 Timothy 1:10). If we stay faithful and do not fall away, we too will one day eat from that tree, as mankind did before the Fall (Revelation 22:14).

The second tree somehow initiated man into the realm of sin. The knowledge about evil wasn't mere technical knowledge, but *experiential* knowledge (Romans 16:19). This was strictly hands off, taboo, *prohibido*, nix, *verboten*, okay to eat—not!

> [10]*A river watering the garden flowed from Eden; from there it was separated into four headwaters.* [11]*The name of the first is the Pishon; it winds through the entire land of Havilah, where there is gold.* [12]*(The gold of that land is good; aromatic resin and onyx are also there.)* [13]*The name of the second river is the Gihon; it winds through the entire land of Cush.* [14]*The name of the third river is the Tigris; it runs along the east side of Asshur. And the fourth river is the Euphrates.*

We have already discussed the Tigris and Euphrates. Many tributaries feed into them. The Pishon and Gihon are obscure; their precise locations are unknown.[13] Some commentators have suggested that the rivers are not to be understood geographically.[14] While this interpretation is possible, it certainly is not compelling.

> [15]*The LORD God took the man and put him in the Garden of Eden to work it and take care of it.*

God placed man in the Garden *to work*. It appeals to our lazy, fleshly nature to daydream of a "paradise" where we never have to work at anything; instead, floating around in the clouds, we can do whatever we feel like. If Eden gives us any inkling of what heaven could be like, we certainly won't be idle! Anyway, how could what is sin on earth (see 2 Thessalonians 3:10) be acceptable in heaven?

> [16]*And the LORD God commanded the man, "You are free to eat from any tree in the garden;* [17]*but you must not eat from the tree of the knowledge of good and evil, for when you eat of it you will surely die."*

Here we find a negative command: Man was not allowed to eat from one of the two main trees. Evidently Adam taught Eve this rule, since she is familiar with it in 3:1. God warns that if they eat from this tree they will die (2:17).[15] Physical death, not just "spiritual" death, seems to be in mind. Though God "delays" the sentence, Adam does eventually expire, age 930 (Genesis 5:5).[16]

> [18]*The LORD God said, "It is not good for the man to be alone. I will make a helper suitable for him."*
>
> [19]*Now the LORD God had formed out of the ground all the beasts of the field and all the birds of the air. He brought them to the man to see what he would name them; and whatever the man called each living creature, that was its name.* [20]*So the man gave names to all the livestock, the birds of the air and all the beasts of the field.*
>
> *But for Adam no suitable helper was found.* [21]*So the LORD God caused the man to fall into a deep sleep; and while he was sleeping, he took one of the man's ribs and closed up the place with flesh.* [22]*Then the LORD God made a woman from the rib he had taken out of the man, and he brought her to the man.*

It is not good for man to be alone! If you're single, take God at his word![17] Much could be said on this, and much will be said in our chapter on sexuality and marriage.

The naming of the animals *could* extend to all animals on the planet earth, but this is unlikely, for several reasons:

- The "beasts of the field" are animals related to agriculture. Livestock are also mentioned. Cattle, sheep and goats seem to be what the Genesis writer had in mind. No mention is made of "beasts of the forest" or other animals who would need to be named in a universal naming session.
- Fish are conspicuously excluded, though their creation is mentioned (Day 5).[18]
- The sheer number of species to be named (in the millions) would prohibit this.
- The purpose of Adam's meeting the animals was to locate a suitable companion. ("But for Adam no suitable helper was found.")
- The writer is making the general point that man names the animals (not the other way around) because he has dominion over them (1:28).

[23]*The man said,*

"This is now bone of my bones
  and flesh of my flesh;
she shall be called 'woman,'
  for she was taken out of man."

[24]*For this reason a man will leave his father and mother and be united to his wife, and they will become one flesh.*
[25]*The man and his wife were both naked, and they felt no shame.*

Man meets woman for the first time.[19] The first impression? "Bone of my bones and flesh of my flesh": Adam felt physically and emotionally close to her! The meaning of the Hebrew is much more like our expressions, "Ah hah!" or "Wow!" Reading between the lines, it was immediately thereafter that Adam was united to his new wife.

The Bible clearly teaches that sex is only for marriage. Sexual union is authorized between man and wife. Not only that, cohabitation is only for married couples. At marriage a man *leaves* his previous living arrangement to reside with his bride.[20] Genesis is clear: Sexuality is by no means an afterthought! Everything God created is good (in the proper context, of course), and sexuality is part of God's original creation.

At this point mankind had not fallen. The man and woman were enjoying life with their Creator in the pristine garden of Eden. There was, in fact, no need for redemption, no need for a Savior. And there was no shame. At the dawn of mankind's sojourn on the earth, evil had not infected the world. Wonderfully and amazingly, no one had sinned and fallen short of the glory of God (Romans 3:23).[21] Not yet.

Top Secret!

Eden is a "secret garden" for several reasons. It is secret in a physical sense in that no one seems to be able to locate it. It is secret in a spiritual sense in that only the initiated can understand the words spoken of it. And it is secret in an emotional sense in that, this side of the grave, our wildest dreams only faintly conceive the wonders God has prepared for us in paradise.

Notes

1. The name *Eden* comes from the Sumerian originally, and later became *'edinu* in Akkadian (the language of Assyria and Babylon). It is possible that *edinu* is related to the word for "plain."

2. An engaging question arises: Is Eden to be understood in the same way with respect to the *initial* state of the children of God as Revelation 21-22 is with respect to their *final* state? Would we not be more consistent to interpret both Eden and the New Jerusalem as figures which point to a deeper historic reality? There are three basic possibilities regarding Eden and the account of Adam and Eve:

- They are purely *mythical*. This is the view of most theologians. I remember well being derided by a fellow student at divinity school when I told him I believed in an historical Adam! Yet as Christians we must reject the mythical view, since the NT writers understood them to be historical. By "mythical" we do not mean "containing elements of symbolism"—both communion and baptism contain symbolic elements, yet there is nothing "fictitious" about them!— but "of the nature of, consisting of, or based on purely fictitious narrative(s) usually involving supernatural persons, actions, or events,

and embodying some popular idea concerning natural or historical phenomena" (Oxford Dictionary).
- Every detail is meant to be taken as *literal*. This is possible, but the burden of proof would be on the exegete, who would be swimming against a stream of interpretation (both liberal and conservative) that has flowed since the early days of the church. This may be the simplest view, yet there are numerous problems that arise with it.
- They are *symbolic and historical*. Adam, Eve, Satan, Eden and so on truly existed, yet the account is couched in symbolic language. For a NT parallel, see Revelation 12, where the woman clothed with the sun is the church, Satan is the dragon, and after the birth of a male child (Christ) the woman is protected in the desert—symbolizing God's faithfulness to his persecuted saints. I know of no scholar who takes these details as literal. Yet John is patently describing historical realities in the 1st century.

The biblical theme of paradise will be explored at length in Appendix E.

3. Or does it? The Bible never says it was destroyed. In Revelation 2:7 it is still open to those who approach it without sin (that is, those who are clothed with Christ).

4. "North by east," to be precise. If it is objected that the writer would have said "north" if Eden were located in Turkey, see Genesis 11:2, where mankind moves "east" to *Shinar* (Babylon). This presumes people migrated from the region of the mountains of Ararat (Genesis 8:4) and that the Table of Nations (Genesis 10) chronologically belongs after chapter 11. On this subject scholarly debate continues.

5. "Mesopotamia" is literally "[the land] between the rivers," from *mesos,* "amidst," and *potamos,* "river."

6. Topography, coastlines and the courses of rivers in the Middle East have changed tremendously even since the time of Christ, and this should prevent us from being overly dogmatic *vis-à-vis* the identification of some ancient locations. For example, radar images show clearly underground features—rivers, human settlements long since covered over, and the contours of a once lush landscape—in the Arabian peninsula, much of which used to be grassy savanna. (Alexander Stille, *Farsighted Tools Bring Ruins into Focus,* Washington Post, A-3: 2 September 1996.)

7. It is speculated (Ernest Lucas, *Genesis Today)* that the city Cain built (Genesis 4:17) was *Çatal Hüyük,* dating from 8000 B.C., located in the part of Turkey suggested by the Eden account. *Çatal Hüyük* had a religious sanctuary, showing that religion was a significant part of the life of mankind 10,000 years ago! For more information on the beginning of civilization in the Near East, see Trevor Watkins' *Pushing back the Frontiers of Mesopotamian Prehistory,* Biblical Archaeologist 76-181, December 1992. The entire issue is titled *The Cradle of Civilization: Recent Archaeology in Iraq.* See also "The Rivers of Eden?" *in Biblical Archaeological Review,* November-December, 1996, p. 15. For the view that Eden was in Africa which identifies the Pishon and the Gihon as the Blue and White Nile respectively, see *The Macmillan Bible Atlas* (New York: Macmillan Publishing, 1993), p. 21.

8. It is interesting that nowhere does the Bible imply Eden is a place someone could locate or travel to. Perhaps because paradise can never be found on

a physical map—only by means of a spiritual one! Maybe this is the reason we are unable to locate four intersecting rivers in our (modern or ancient) atlas!

9. For example, the generic *Adam* means "mankind," while *Adamah* means "ground" (see 2:7). *Eve*, the mother of the living, means "living" (3:20). (The word for "a man" is 'i_, related to 'i__ah, the word for "woman"; see 2:23.) Many names in Genesis are deeply symbolic. Now one might argue that something symbolic is not historical. This would be false reasoning. To take one example, *Immanuel* (Isaiah 7:14) means "God [is] with us," yet no one would reason that the child isn't an actual human being!

10. Technically all of the Middle East belongs to western Asia.

11. We read that God hadn't sent rain on the "earth." The word *'erets* can mean *earth* but it more often means *land,* which would in this case refer to the part of the Near East inhabited by original man.

12. Though I confess biologically speaking I am a (true) carnivore!

13. There is a possibility that the Pishon is a subterranean extension of the Kuwait River, as suggested persuasively in a *The River Runs Dry* by James A. Sauer, featured in *Biblical Archaeological Review,* Vol. 22, No. 4, 1996. This informative article argues convincingly that the entire area from the Arabian Peninsula northward was, during the period 7500-3500 B.C., quite wet, and during this time the Kuwait River flowed aboveground without interruption nearly the whole way to Medina. Of course if Sauer is correct, the suggestion of an Iraqi location for Eden is greatly strengthened.

14. Some Greek sources call the Nile the *Gichôn*. If the Pishon could be identified with the Indus, the four great rivers supporting life in the ancient world would have been represented—strengthening their case.

15. In 2:17 "when" (NIV) is literally "in the day." For a parallel which helps us understand how Adam was to die in the day he violated the command, see 1 Kings 2:36-46 in the KJV. We see that he was, effectively, placed under a death sentence from the point of his disobedience.

16. We will take up the question of the long life spans in Chapter 12.

17. Assuming you don't possess the rather rare gift of celibacy! 1 Corinthians 7:7ff shows there are definite benefits to celibacy. Yet celibacy is a *gift* from God (as is a spouse—Proverbs 18:22!) and this being the case, no one can bind celibacy on others (1 Timothy 4:3; 1 Corinthians 9:5; Hebrews 13:4).

18. Nor is any mention made of insects, spiders, microscopic organisms, or other creatures!

19. And what did he say? "Madam in Eden, I'm Adam": that is, if he spoke in palindromes (words and sentences that read the same backwards as forward)!

20. Genesis 2:24 is a handy verse to use in studying the Bible with our friends: easy to find, easy to understand.

21. For an enjoyable, if speculative, book on life before the Fall—in this case on the planet Venus—read C. S. Lewis' *Perelandra*.

7
The Better Half

Woman

Scripture makes it perfectly clear that the creation of woman is not an afterthought. God created in his image: male and female (Genesis 1:27). Woman is just as much a special part of God's creation as man. However, the prevailing attitude in the world toward women has always been tragic. The Qur'an[1] teaches that Allah made men superior to women, and that unruly wives are to be rebuked, sent to bed and beaten![2] The Apocrypha (officially accepted as Scripture by nearly a billion people today) states "The birth of a daughter is a loss."[3] A popular Chinese proverb calls baby girls "maggots in the rice bowl."[4] Tens of millions of women on the earth are routinely abused, shouted at, sworn at, bullied, and beaten every day.

But, in God's eyes there is nothing second-class about women. The heart of God cannot properly be apprehended without an appreciation of woman.

Is God Male?

So should we think of God as male? Every passage in the Bible that bears on the subject encourages us to relate to God as a Father.[5] If this agitates the feminists among us, let me remind you that in the Bible all of us stand (corporately) in a *female* relationship to God! (Ephesians 5:22-32). The fatherhood of God has the direct support of Jesus himself, who

Answering Accusations of "Chauvinism"

Many critics of Christianity allege that biblical faith is unfair toward women. Here are a few practical replies to these allegations:

- Jesus had great friendships with men and women alike. In Luke 8:3 we see many women so enthusiastic about his message that they financially supported his ministry!
- Contrary to popular belief, the apostle Peter was a married man. One of Jesus' earliest miracles was to heal his mother-in-law! (Mark 1:31).
- In the apostle Paul's letters, around 40% of his personal greetings are to women.
- Submission is two-way; Ephesians 5:21 is not invalidated by marriage. This doesn't mean the husband is not to be the spiritual leader, but a good leader often submits to those whom he is leading.
- Most women don't mind male leadership when they are treated with love, sensitivity and respect.
- In the book of Acts we see numbers of prominent women being converted: educated, opinionated women who would never have been won to a "chauvinistic"[6] faith.
- Females, newborns in particular, were treated very poorly in the ancient world.[7]
- Christian principles have elevated the position of women substantially in a world full of religions repressive of women. Would you care to be a woman in India? China? Pakistan? Chad? Iran?[8] Female disciples preach the Word in all these countries; we cannot help but admire them.

taught us to pray "Our Father..." (Matthew 6; Luke 11). God is, strictly speaking, neither male nor female, nor androgynous (both at the same time), but his image is reflected in both male and female. There are several passages that imply that masculinity by itself falls short of the mark, as does femininity, for example 1 Thessalonians 2:6b-12. Perhaps it could be said that *only in the marriage relationship* are the best of male strength and decisiveness and the best of female sensitivity and creativity combined in a godly fusion.

Lonesome Stranger

It is not good for man to be alone! (2:18). Among the animals, no suitable helper was found (2:20), and so woman was created for man—not just to procreate more men. Woman is created for man because man has a deep need, a vacuum in his life. Without her he isn't just a "poor wayfaring stranger." He's a lonesome one, too!

Eve is said to be a "help" to man (2:18). Does this mean she is "inferior"? Not unless God is inferior to mankind! 1 Samuel 7:12 uses the same word "help" (*'ezer*) in speaking of God himself! Eve was created from Adam's "rib" (or "side"). Interestingly, in Arabic culture when one person is very close to another it is said: "He is my rib." (A rough equivalent might be "my better half.") Now whether it was his rib, part of his side, or part of his genes—translators are divided—is irrelevant. God created her, she's man's greatest ally and best friend (after God). As someone quipped, woman came

> Not from his head, to rule over him;
> Not from his foot, to be trodden on by him;
> But from his side, to be his equal.

I am a better man for having married. The number of times my wife's better judgment has convinced me to change my mind is countless. The likelihood that I would have become a counselor, able to empathize with others' feelings had I not been married to Vicki, in my mind, is non-existent! My chances of becoming a happy father of three without *her* were nil!

If you are a married man, or contemplating marriage, never forget the true blessing a woman of God is. If you have grown ungrateful, study Proverbs 31 one morning in your devotions. Then count your blessings. And give an extra hug to your better half!

Notes

1. The 114 surahs of the Qur'an (Koran) are the scriptures of one in five human beings in the world today: over a billion!

2. Qur'an, Surah 4:34.

3. Sirach 22:3. See also Ecclesiasticus 25:13-26:18.

4. China has a population of well over a billion.

5. In Isaiah 66:13, God does not teach us to address him as a mother, but he is not hesitant to say that he deals with his people with the care and compassion of a mother.

6. Strictly speaking, "chauvinism" is "exaggerated and bellicose patriotism" [Oxford Dictionary], but in late-twentieth century parlance, it is acquiring the meaning of misogyny ("woman-hating").

7. Contemporary sociology recognizes the abysmal status and treatment of women in the ancient world, and the utter contrast in which the Christian religion held out true hope to women. In The Rise of Christianity, p. 118 (Princeton: Princeton University Press, 1996) the sociologist Rodney Stark writes:

Both Plato [Republic 5 (1941 ed.)] and Aristotle [Politics, 2,7 (1986 ed.)] recommended infanticide as legitimate state policy. The Twelve Tables — the earliest known Roman legal code, written about 450 B.C.E. — permitted a father to expose any female infant and any deformed or weak male infant (Gorman 1982:25). During recent excavations of a villa in the port city of Ashkelon, Lawrence E. Stager and his colleagues made a gruesome discovery in the sewer that ran under the bathhouse... This sewer had been clogged with refuse sometime in the sixth century A.D. When we excavated and dry-sieved the desiccated sewage, we found [the] bones... of nearly 100 little babies apparently murdered and thrown into the sewer. (1991:47)

Examination of the bones revealed them to be newborns, probably day-olds (Smith and Kahila 1991).

8. In "democratic" India, which is over 80% Hindu, opportunities for its 470 million women are limited, indeed. Hinduism teaches that you get in this life what you earned in the last; a certain fatalism and passivity is not, therefore, entirely unexpected. Wife-beating and spousal abuse are rampant. A disgrace in the history of India is *suttee* (the burning alive of a Hindu widow with her husband). Although the practice is less common these days than in

the nineteenth century, it still occurs in India.

With the official "one-child" policy, authorities often force women to abort, or "terminate," the newborn infant, and exact heavy fines from persons exceeding the one-child limit. China is officially atheist, though Taoism-Buddhism survives in many parts. Until the revolution of 1911, women's feet were commonly "bound" (wrapped so tightly that their shape became grossly distorted and nearly useless for walking) all because men preferred women with smaller feet!

Pakistan severely restricts the freedom of women. Women are not allowed on the streets at night. This is a radical Islamic republic. In another Muslim nation, Saudi Arabia, women are not allowed to drive cars.

Female circumcision is becoming an international issue. Such nations as Chad, Somalia and the Sudan show unspeakable cruelty toward their female citizens in perpetuating this barbaric ritual, first recorded in Egypt more than 4,000 years ago. Much of Muslim or tribalistic Africa enforces this rite of passage.

If these comments are hard to relate to, rent a copy of the film *Not Without My Daughter* and prepare to see how women are treated in many countries of the world (in this case the fundamentalist Islamic republic of Iran). In short, women's rights are virtually non-existent. If you are saving up for a trip abroad, why not consider the Third World? The trip can be not only recreational, but also educational. You may never complain about your "Western" problems again!

8

Till Death Do Us Part

Sexuality and Marriage

Human sexuality was created by God, and everything God created is good (Genesis 1:31). Hence sexuality is good. It may come as a surprise that sex was not the discovery of man, a sort of Promethean fire stolen from the gods.[1] It was God's gift and plan for his children. You don't have to wait until the twenty-second book of the Bible (Song of Songs) to find sexual love—it's found in the first couple of pages of God's word! The LORD did not want us to miss the point, or miss out on the blessings of marriage.

Sexuality was one of the more "daring" aspects of God's creation, since there is such a chance it may be misused. Yet, as long as sexuality isn't abused, it has a glorious place: in the marriage relationship. Yes, the principle of "one wife for life" has always been the will of God. In this chapter we examine the theme of sexuality in Genesis.

Sex in the Bible

What does God's word have to say on the subject? How comprehensive are the Scriptures? We will limit our discussion to what the book of Genesis has to say.

First of all, marriage is the time a man and a woman should begin living together, as well as enter sexual union, according to Genesis 2:24. This is a practical verse—use it as you teach your friends.

Some religious groups teach that the "forbidden fruit" was sex! But that view is dead wrong![2] Adam and Eve had already been commanded to "be fruitful and multiply."[3] The traditional view attaches shame to one of God's good gifts for married couples.

Romance

Romance must have a spiritual basis. Marriage should not be entered primarily on the basis of physical attraction.[4] The world got into a total mess when men married for lust, rather than for love (In the commentary on Genesis 6:2 we will elaborate more on this). If you are single, are you getting good advice in this area (and taking it)?

Compare Genesis 29 with Genesis 34. Jacob and Shechem had totally different approaches to getting a wife. Shechem's "love" (Genesis 34:3) did not somehow negate his immorality (34:2). Feelings *never* justify illicit sex. What a contrast Jacob's godly approach is! He waited seven years and seven days before beginning life with the wife of his choice, the apple of his eye![5]

Needless to say, our world is hopelessly confused about romance. Popular songs fill the airwaves with lyrics of lust and love lost. Even the word "love" has become a virtual synonym for sex.

And the confusion has hit the denominational world equally hard. I well remember the advice of one of my university professors to his class. His fatherly counsel was to get a girlfriend or boyfriend, since romance would help us be more rounded as students, and "make love" three times a week. He was a Sunday school teacher in a local church.

Whose advice are you going to take? God's or the world's? The world includes worldly religion, for it is true that when the church is not converting the world, the world will convert the church.

What Constitutes Marriage?

When, in God's eyes, is a couple married? When they

> ## Terms
>
> Monogamy   Marriage to one partner
> Polygamy[6]   Marriage to more than one partner
> Fornication   Any sex outside the sphere of marriage
> Adultery   Sexual sin involving one or more
>   persons not married to each other
> Immorality   Sin, not necessarily sexual
> Lust   Sexual desire dwelt upon, which has
>   "conceived" (James 1:13-15)

first love each other? At engagement? When they sleep together and "consummate" the relationship? When their license is signed? First and foremost, marriage is a *legal* institution and as such, is defined by the state. Laws vary from nation to nation.[7] In earliest times the patriarchal law was supreme and dictated the terms of marriage.[8] Once again, traditions and ceremonies do not define marriage; the law does.

It should be said that in biblical times (and even not so long ago!) marriage involved the whole society. It was a public event. In modern times marriage has become a private affair; some persons opt for a civil service, the social aspect of the ceremony being kept to a bare minimum. This is a direct result of two factors: individualism (emphasis on self) and the breakdown of community.

The Polygamy Issue

Lamech (Genesis 4:19) and Jacob, (Genesis 29)[9] had more than one wife, which defines polygamy. In fact the Old Testament does *not* approve of polygamy, but rather implicitly teaches the opposite: all polygamous marriages are strife-torn ones. This is well illustrated in the book of Genesis, as in the rest of the Old Testament. Each man who took more than one wife had to bear the consequences!

In New Testament times men with multiple wives were automatically disqualified from the eldership (1 Timothy 3:2; Titus 1:6). Today in most countries, polygamy is illegal. In those countries where it is not, these verses from the Pastoral epistles take on a special meaning! In case anyone missed it, God's plan has *always* been one wife for life.

Sexual Sins

God takes the sin of adultery with the utmost seriousness. Genesis 20 shows how radically God is prepared to deal with this sin—even if it is "accidental." Not only adultery, but most of the sexual sins specified by the Law[10] are dealt with in Genesis, in the lives of the patriarchs.

Temptation strikes hard in Genesis 39. Joseph resisted well, to the point of unjust imprisonment. How well do we resist Satan's attacks? Do we fend them off or nonchalantly embrace them? The tempter may not come for you as boldly as Potiphar's wife—at least not through another person—but he may come blatantly for you through scantily clad women or men in the workplace, through television (especially watch out if you have cable TV), through Internet browsing, or through magazines or books.

Prostitution, of course, is against God's will (Genesis 38:24)[11] as is homosexuality. This sin is roundly condemned in both testaments (Genesis 19; Romans 1:27). The sin of *sodomy* (once a criminal offense) is named after the perverse residents of Sodom. Moreover, Ham's sin seems to have involved homosexual lust (Genesis 9:22).

Certain psychologists, "experts" in sexuality, rights activists and a host of others do a great disservice to gays and lesbians by trying to convince the public (*à la* Romans 1:32), including those personally participating in homosexual activities, that this sin is somehow natural. It is anything but

Twelve Practical Passages on Sexual Sin

Genesis 2:24
Marriage and then sexual union are God's plan. You move in with your spouse only once married. "Leaving," then "cleaving."

Genesis 29:20-21
Intercourse only after marriage; patience, not experimentation for "compatibility." In Eden homosexuality, incest and adultery were all demographically impossible!

Job 31:1
Be careful what you allow your eyes to see!

Proverbs 5-7
God warns us to watch out especially for sexual sin.

John 4:18
It is wrong to live with someone to whom you're not married.

Romans 1:24-27
Homosexuality is not God's plan for your life.

1 Corinthians 6:9-11
We can overcome any sin, sexual sin included.

1 Corinthians 6:12-20
Your body belongs to God; be careful what you do with it.

Titus 2:11-12
God's grace enables to say "no" to any sin.

Hebrews 13:4
Sex is only for the marriage bed.

1 Peter 4:3-4
Worldly life-styles tend to revolve around sensual indulgence.

Revelation 21:8
Sexual sin will do more than ruin you in this life; it will destroy you in the next.[12]

natural, unless by "natural" we mean serving self or following the path of least resistance—which is indeed the way of the world (Genesis 4:7, 1 John 2:15-17).

Homosexual sin, like any other sin, can be overcome, just as much today as in the early church. (Be inspired and encouraged by 1 Corinthians 6:9-11!) The Holy Spirit (Romans 6-8) helps us to put sin to death.

Any time we abuse God's gifts, we hurt ourselves. Sexuality is like eating, drinking, sleeping, games, even reading, which all are good things but must be used properly. If they are misused, the results are devastating: perversion, obesity, drunkenness, laziness, flippancy, unrelatability.

Remember this: lust toppled the wisest man, the strongest man, and the purest man. Solomon, Samson and David all alike shared that fatal flaw.[13]

The Need for Companionship

I have often walked through a cemetery, sometimes just to be alone and think, other times to pray. It never fails to move me to see a child's grave. In the same way, it always seems somehow right that a man and his wife are buried side by side. Yet it is painful for me to see the grave of a man without a wife buried alongside his dog. Not that I have anything against dogs—as a child I enjoyed playing with all of our dogs. But a dog was not created by God to be "man's best friend." Woman was.[14]

There is something good, right and wholesome about finding your companion. "He who finds a wife finds what is good and receives favor from the Lord" (Proverbs 18:22).

Get Married!

God's plan is incredible, and so important that in revealing his heart to us in Genesis, he conveyed the marriage plan right after the Creation. Don't have the attitude of Lady Astor, who said, "I married beneath me. All women do." Female chauvinism is no less attractive than male chauvinism! We

were not created to be independent of one another. Unless
you have the (rare) gift of celibacy (Matthew 19:12), God has
a plan for your life. It involves a husband or wife!

The divorce rate in the United States is painfully high. Yet
among former live-in lovers, who account for a huge part of
all couples, the rate is even higher.[15] In the opinion of the
author, in a sense, 95% of all marriages end in divorce—divorce in the heart. God's beautiful plan ends up being per-
verted into something horrible. Couples have no one outside
of their marriage to talk to about it, and when they do go to
professionals, they are as likely to get bad advice as good. A
sense of doom and entrapment descends over the relationship, and expectations are mutually, gradually lowered, with
couples settling for a relationship that, as youths, they vowed
they would never allow.[16] For them, the words of Mae West
sadly come true: "Marriage is a great institution—but I'm not
ready for an institution." When disciples speak of the institution of marriage, they speak of it with awe. Not because it is
awful, but because it is so *awesome.*

Let's be determined to get back to the word of God and
his perfect plan. That's *one man for one wife for life![17]*

Notes

1. In the Greek myth, Prometheus, son of the Titan Iapetus, made man out
of clay, stole fire from Olympus, and taught men how to use it. His punishment was a horrible torture: Zeus chained him to a rock, where his liver was
eaten every day by a vulture.

2. This misunderstanding is perpetuated by the Apocrypha: for example,
in the books of Tobit [Latin version] and [the additions to] Esther.

3. Sex is declared by the Catholic Church to be legitimate only for procre-
ation, not "recreation." Yet this is unbiblical; the Bible has a whole book of
(sexual) love poetry for marrieds: the Song of Solomon.

4. Genesis 24 illustrates this principle magnificently. Isaac delegates the
selection of his bride to a trusted servant. She is chosen on the basis of her
religious purity and trustworthiness, with virtually no regard to "personality"
or "looks"—although Isaac was not short-changed in these departments either. The marriage is entered and sustained successfully—a total refutation of
the "enlightened" notion that spirituality is a secondary consideration, "sexual
compatibility" being the primary factor in a relationship. Our society's track

record on divorce, separation and unhappy marriages only drives us to the wisdom of the Bible.

5. Much more about Jacob and his complex marital situation will be covered in the sequel to this book: *The God Who Dared, Vol II: Abraham to Egypt.*

6. There are two varieties of polygamy: *polygyny* (one man, multiple wives) and the rarer practice of *polyandry* (one woman, multiple husbands). *Bigamy* is marriage to *two* persons.

7. Marriage must be internationally recognized. If you meet someone who claims to be married, ask whether this is reflected in official documents, such as passports, or was merely a family agreement, lacking any basis in law.

My wife and I were married in England, under the laws of the U.K. We were first legally man and wife when the presiding minister finalized the marriage certificate, all parties having duly affixed their signatures thereunto. If you had a civil ceremony, but deferred living together until a "church" wedding, nothing was changed: you were still married (in God's eyes) when the civil procedures were completed! We must follow the laws of the land—not, of course, common customs.

8. "In pastoral nomadic groups the father is the absolute master of his own family and has complete legal control over them. He arranges marriages, conducts all business transactions and serves as the sole source of justice in legal matters involving his family." (Source: Victor H. Matthews, *Manners and Customs in the Bible,* Peabody, Massachusetts: Hendrickson, 1992, p.30.) The patriarchal legal arrangement pertains to much of Genesis.

9. Hagar (Genesis 16) is a *concubine,* or *secondary* wife; concubinage was widespread in the ancient world. Archaeological research illustrates the practice, common in Abraham's time, of siring a child through a maidservant in the event of the barrenness of the wife.

10. As in, for example, Leviticus 18.

11. Note the double standard: Prostitution is no less wrong for the man, although his authority enabled him to escape consequences.

12. Other helpful passages which address the subject of sexual immorality are Genesis 39:9; Exodus 20:14, 22:16; Leviticus 18; Numbers 25:1-9; Deuteronomy 22:13-30; Ezekiel 16, 23; Habakkuk 2:15; Matthew 5:28, 15:19; Mark 6:18, 7:21; Romans 6-7, 13:14; 1 Corinthians 5, 10:8; 2 Corinthians 12:21; Galatians 5:19; Ephesians 5:3-7; Colossians 3:5; 1 Thessalonians 4:3-8; 1 Timothy 5:2; 2 Timothy 2:22; 1 Peter 2:11; 2 Peter 2:14; Jude 7-8 and Revelation 2:21, 9:21, 21:27, 22:15.

13. Study 2 Samuel, in which we read of the tragic legacy of sexual sin in the family of David; Judges 13-16, in which we see the effects of lust on the man Samson; and 1 Kings 11:1-13, where we read of the effects of this sin on the life of Solomon.

14. Yes, our society is so dysfunctional that it's increasingly the case that a man is more likely to stand by his dog than his wife—and the dog may more consistently receive fair treatment!

15. Official statistics do not include the damage done by "live-in lovers" who end up abandoning one another—and often the children left in their wake. In our first apartment block in Stockholm, exactly half of the couples were married.

16. The commonly heard statement that there is a 50% divorce rate in the United States is not accurate. In some years there has been one divorce for approximately every two *new* marriages, but that does not mean that half of all those who marry end up divorced. More careful studies indicate that approximately 20% of those who have been married have also been divorced. However, since the 1970s there has been a surge in the divorce rate. According to the U.S. National Center for Health Statistics, in one out of seven marriages either the bride or the groom is marrying for the *third* time. This is double the rate of 1970.

17. Highly recommended is *Friends and Lovers: Marriage as God Designed It* by Sam and Geri Laing (Woburn, Mass.: Discipleship Publications International, 1996).

Daring in Re-Creation

Four times God provides a fresh start:
after the Rebellion, the Murder, the Flood and
the Tower. The New Testament doctrine
of the new creation (2 Corinthians 5:17) is not
totally new. God, in the Old Testament, had shown
his willingness, over and over again,
to dare to create anew.

9

The Father of Lies

The Fall from Grace

Lying is destructive. "The lying tongue hates those it hurts," as Solomon noted (Proverbs 26:28). Yet lies about the word of God are most destructive. They can destroy our souls. This is precisely what Satan successfully did to Adam and Eve in the Garden—and millennia later he even tried to dupe Jesus Christ (Matthew 4). The Lord called Satan "the father of lies" (John 8:44). Rather humorously he declared, "When he lies, he speaks his native language"!

If you are reading this book fairly rapidly, your native language is probably English. Do you speak any others? Although I read ten languages, I must confess that I am fluent only in two of them: Swedish and English. Fluency means it flows; you don't have to search for the words, because you know them. What languages is Satan fluent in? Oh yes, Beelzebub speaks the thousands of languages of mankind—but only "as a second language." His first language is lying, and he has spoken it for so long that he can hardly distinguish truth from lie anymore. For he is indeed the father of lies.

> *3:1Now the serpent was more crafty than any of the wild animals the LORD God had made. He said to the woman, "Did God really say, 'You must not eat from any tree in the garden'?"*
>
> *2The woman said to the serpent, "We may eat fruit from the trees in the garden, 3but God did say, 'You must not eat fruit from*

the tree that is in the middle of the garden, and you must not touch
it, or you will die.'"

Presumably the snake[1] waited for the opportune moment
before striking.[2] His approach: to cause Eve to doubt God's
word. This is the subterfuge Jesus refers to in John 8. Notice
how Satan twists and misquotes what God says—like so many
religious charlatans today!

What is your best defense against the onslaught of Satan,
and against the error of false teachers? It is to know the Bible.
Embody the attitudes of Psalm 119; saturate yourself in the
word of God. If you do not set aside some time on a daily
basis to study the Word, you may be easier prey for the devil
than you realize!

> [4] *"You will not surely die," the serpent said to the woman.* [5] *"For*
> *God knows that when you eat of it your eyes will be opened, and*
> *you will be like God, knowing good and evil."*

Here the Adversary drops subtlety and attacks the Word
head-on, bringing into question God's motives and God's security! Satan tries to "cut God down to size" in Eve's eyes. Our
generation is coming more and more to disbelieve in a transcendent, almighty God. In a popular '90s song "One of Us"[3]
the singer wonders: "What if God was one of us? Just a slob like
one of us? Just a stranger on the bus, tryin' to make his way
home?" Can you see what is happening here? It's not that we are
really doubting whether there is a God, it's that we are "cutting
him down to size," and we are trying to set ourselves up as
gods. Really, all we're doing is setting ourselves up for disaster!

By the way, the forbidden fruit, which is unspecified, is
no apple.[4] Nor is it something sexual.[5] It is a the fruit of
experiential knowledge of good and evil.[6]

So how does Satan attack God's word in your life? There
are so many ways the devil causes us to doubt. Consider a few:

Doubts

So how does Satan attack God's word in your life? There are

so many ways the devil causes us to doubt. Consider a few:
- Maybe there isn't a God—it's all in our heads!...
- Do I really *have* to be this committed? Maybe I *was* saved before....
- Surely it doesn't matter if I miss church now and again....
- Does the Bible really teach that I can marry only a disciple?...
- Maybe there's another verse somewhere showing an easier way....
- How can such a nice person *not* be right with God?...
- Maybe there *aren't* any answers to my questions....
- Maybe there's no connection between my selfishness and my ineffectiveness....
- Maybe God doesn't love me as much as he loves *so and so*....

We know that the Bible is true. So what we need to do, as is often preached, is to make a decision. We need to decide to stop doubting our beliefs and believing our doubts, and start doubting our doubts and believing our beliefs.

> *⁶When the woman saw that the fruit of the tree was good for food and pleasing to the eye, and also desirable for gaining wisdom, she took some and ate it. She also gave some to her husband, who was with her, and he ate it. ⁷Then the eyes of both of them were opened, and they realized they were naked; so they sewed fig leaves together and made coverings for themselves.*

Forbidden Fruit

Even though they were tempted by the snake ("The devil made me do it"!), God took their sin seriously—it was *rebellion*. All sin is fundamentally insisting on doing things our way instead of God's way.⁷ They had free will, and so do we.

The text says Adam was with Eve when she was tempted. What a weak leader he was! He watched it all, but did not take a stand for what he knew was right. We need strong, godly marriages where the husband does not "wimp out." How is your marriage? Do your children totally respect your spirituality? Do they want to be just like you? (Because they probably will be.)

> *⁸Then the man and his wife heard the sound of the LORD God as he was walking in the garden in the cool of the day, and they hid from the LORD God among the trees of the garden. ⁹But the LORD God called to the man, "Where are you?"*
>
> *¹⁰He answered, "I heard you in the garden, and I was afraid because I was naked; so I hid."*
>
> *¹¹And he said, "Who told you that you were naked? Have you eaten from the tree that I commanded you not to eat from?"*
>
> *¹²The man said, "The woman you put here with me - she gave me some fruit from the tree, and I ate it."*
>
> *¹³Then the LORD God said to the woman, "What is this you have done?"*
>
> *The woman said, "The serpent deceived me, and I ate."*

The Bitter Fruit of Sin

Notice the effects of sin (this pattern will reappear in the life of Cain):

1. Separation from God. The relationship is affected.
2. Hiding, pretending, playing games (3:8).
3. Blame-shifting (3:12-13). Adam has a negative attitude toward both his wife and God.
4. Life becomes burdensome (3:16-19).

Despite all its allure and false appeal to "freedom," nothing about sin brings the slightest improvement to our lives. Why did we ever doubt the word of God?

The Three-Fold Curse

The triple curse (3:14-19) follows the rebellion of mankind. This is the historic Fall. Romans 5:12-21 is one of the classic New Testament passages explaining what truly happened in the Garden. Like a Level Four hot virus, sin spread to all men, though we are not told how it spread. Only the Bible gives a reasonable explanation for how and why the world is as it has become: The *how* is human sin, the *why* is the historic Fall of mankind.

*[14]So the LORD God said to the serpent, "Because you have done
this,*

> *Cursed are you above all the livestock
>   and all the wild animals!
> You will crawl on your belly
>   and you will eat dust
>   all the days of your life.
> [15]And I will put enmity
>   between you and the woman,
>   and between your offspring and hers;
> he will crush your head,
>   and you will strike his heel."*

[16]To the woman he said,

> *"I will greatly increase your pains in childbearing;
>   with pain you will give birth to children.
> Your desire will be for your husband,
>   and he will rule over you."*

*[17]To Adam he said, "Because you listened to your wife and ate
from the tree about which I commanded you, 'You must not eat of
it,'*

> *"Cursed is the ground because of you;
>   through painful toil you will eat of it
>   all the days of your life.
> [18]It will produce thorns and thistles for you,
>   and you will eat the plants of the field.
> [19]By the sweat of your brow
>   you will eat your food
> until you return to the ground,
>   since from it you were taken;
> for dust you are
>   and to dust you will return."*

First God curses the snake. The slithering serpent reap-
pears as a great dragon in Revelation 12. In 3:15 we find the
first Messianic prophecy in the Bible.[8] The Christ will crush
the head of Satan, though Satan will wound him ("strike his

heel") at Golgotha. (See also Revelation 12:17; Romans 16:20.) God had planned the redemption of the Cross from the very beginning (1 Peter 1:20).[9]

God addresses the woman second. Her labor pains are to be "greatly increased. " Does this not imply that she had given birth before?[10] (More will be said on this in Chapter 11.) In addition, her relationship with her husband is affected.[11] Not surprisingly, sin affects marriages. The woman is punished where it hurts most: in the domestic arena. Both childbirth and marriage are cursed.

Finally God addresses the man. Man (Adam) is hit where it hurts: his career. He will have to work harder, and his relationship with nature will not be as harmonious as at the beginning. The true meaning of his name is to be realized ('adam = "man," 'adamah = "ground") as he is forced to work even closer to the very earth[12]—the same earth from which he came and to which he will surely return, now that he has lost immortality. For the ground he struggles with every day as a farmer will one day overcome him.

Reverse that Curse!

Things were never to be the same again, now that mankind had rebelled against his Creator. He had fallen.[13] The age of innocence had ended. This is what inevitably happens when we listen to the father of lies.

Yet there is good news: the curse is *reversed* in Jesus Christ (Romans 7:24-8:39; Galatians 3:13). Although sin mars the creation of God, the Lord, in his grace, is always willing to "re-create," to give us a fresh start. And one day we will, in a way not yet clearly revealed, revisit Eden as we enter paradise (Revelation 2:7).

Notes

1. The pagan snake was a figure well known to the Israelites. In ancient religions, it was not the abhorrent reptile we think of today, but something attractive, beneficial. It represented life, healing and health, as in the Greek Asklepios cult. (Even today, the staff of the American Medical Association, as

well as the British Medical Association, has a snake coiled around it.) It was a giver of power and secret knowledge. The snake represents the attraction of pagan religion and its magic and is also an emblem of the fertility cults, which used ritual prostitution, both male and female, to ensure success of agriculture. There are many references to fertility cult prostitution in the Old Testament, such as Deuteronomy 23:17-18.

2. How much time elapsed between 2:25 and 3:1? We simply don't know how long they were in Eden.

3. By Joan Osborne, nominated for a Grammy Award in 1996. "One of Us" on the CD *Relish* (Polygram Records, 1995).

4. The confusion was occasioned by the Latin Vulgate translation of Genesis, in which *malum* (evil) and *malum* (apple) are homonyms.

5. The traditional interpretation is that the "apple" represents sexual relations. Yet God had already commanded Adam and Eve to "be fruitful and multiply"!

6. See Romans 16:19.

7. This was an inversion of the order established by God in nature: The human is obeying the animal!

8. In the LXX (Septuagint), the third-century-b.c. translation of the Hebrew Bible into Greek, the pronoun in the second half of 3:15 referring to "offspring" is *masculine*. Thus the early Christians, for whom the LXX was the Bible, would have read Genesis 3:15 as a Messianic passage, and so it would have been understood by the receptive Jews and Gentiles with whom they shared the message.

9. There are two Messianic prophecies in Genesis. They are 3:15 and 49:10. Both were considered to foretell the coming of the Christ by the Rabbis of the first century. In addition, there is foreshadowing, such as the remarkable events of Genesis 22. For an in-depth and scholarly approach to the subject, see Satterthwaite, Philip E. et al, *The Lord's Anointed: Interpretation of Old Testament Messianic Texts,* Grand Rapids: Baker, 1995.

10. Perhaps. The same Hebrew phrase occurs in Numbers 26:54 and Job 9:17. In Genesis 3:16 we read literally "multiplying," thus "I will multiply...." Eve need not necessarily already have conceived. On the other hand, this passage, and its likely interpretation, do not rule it out.

11. Scholars have debated the exact meanings of the Hebrew words here translated "desire" and "rule over," and at this point it must be said that the jury is still out.

12. The "dust" to which he must return is the same dust which the serpent will eat; thus the curse of Satan and the curse of man are linked together.

13. This was an historical fall. Biblical writers understood it as such: Hosea 6:7; 2 Corinthians 11:3; 1 Timothy 2:4. If the Fall is myth and not history, then sin never really "entered" the world, we are not responsible, Jesus did not need to come and die, and Christianity is predicated upon a myth.

10

Amazing Grace

The True Heart of God

We saw in the last chapter that things were fundamentally changed once mankind had declared independence, rebelled against the Creator, and fallen from the pristine relationship. Fortunately, the true heart of God is full of compassion.

We all, at some point in our lives, have experienced what Adam experienced and what Eve experienced. We desperately need God's grace,[1] a new beginning. We cry out in desperation, and then in total appreciation,

> *Out of the depths I cry to you, O LORD;*
> *O Lord, hear my voice.*
> *Let your ears be attentive*
> *to my cry for mercy.*
>
> *If you, O LORD, kept a record of sins,*
> *O Lord, who could stand?*
> *But with you there is forgiveness;*
> *therefore you are feared....*
>
> *...put your hope in the LORD,*
> *for with the LORD is unfailing love*
> *and with him is full redemption (Psalm 130:1-7).*

Like the Psalm above, there are many passages in the Bible that praise God for his amazing grace.[2] Grace means that our

sins are not counted against us. Grace means that we are for-
given. Grace means the hope of full redemption. Our response:
reverence, hope, deepest appreciation. Let us resume our study
of Genesis 3:

> [20]*Adam named his wife Eve, because she would become the
> mother of all the living.*
> [21]*The LORD God made garments of skin for Adam and his wife
> and clothed them. [22]And the LORD God said, "The man has now
> become like one of us, knowing good and evil. He must not be al-
> lowed to reach out his hand and take also from the tree of life and
> eat, and live forever."*

After Adam named his wife,[3] the Lord made garments of
skin for them both. (The rather skimpy *fig leaf* apparel just
would not do!) God was protecting them from the elements
to which they would soon be exposed. God says that Adam
and Eve have "become like one of us." This may be the royal
plural, or he may be referring to the angels.

> [23]*So the LORD God banished him from the Garden of Eden to work
> the ground from which he had been taken. [24]After he drove the man
> out, he placed on the east side of the Garden of Eden cherubim and
> a flaming sword flashing back and forth to guard the way to the
> tree of life.*

Cherubim block the way into Eden.[4] God had to block
them from re-entering the Garden, eating of the Tree of Life
and living forever. Why? A rebellious, immortal being bent
on selfishness could wreak havoc in the universe. Can you
imagine what the world would be like if people like Hitler,
Stalin, Idi Amin and Pol Pot were immortal?

God cannot guarantee eternal life to those who have rejected him. This is not to say that Adam and Eve were lost;
God's grace clearly intervened in their lives.

Where then did Adam and Eve go? Surely not the local
Hilton! The best shelter available was probably in a cave![5]
(Where would *you* go?)[6]

Twisted Grace

- A twisted view of God turns grace into a license for sin (Jude 4).
- A twisted view of grace proclaims "faith alone" as sufficient for salvation (see James 2:24).
- A twisted view of faith assures us that we will be saved though we are lukewarm (Revelation 3:14-17).
- A twisted view of salvation makes us keep it to ourselves instead of sharing it with others (Luke 11:23-26).
- A twisted view of others prevents us from seeing them as God sees them (Matthew 25:31-46).

Grace Abundant

Grace was extended to the first couple after their rebellion. They did not die immediately. They were not heartlessly expelled. The LORD took care that they would be able to cope with their new rugged environment.

The truly amazing thing is that this scenario will be repeated three more times in Genesis. There are four major events in which grace is extended (not to mention many, many minor ones):

- Chapter 3: After the rebellion in Eden, God spares Adam and Eve.
- Chapter 4: After the murder of Abel, God spares Cain, giving him a fresh start.
- Chapter 7: In the great Deluge, God spares Noah and his family.
- Chapter 11: At Babel, God again protects man from himself and extends grace.[7]

How Sweet the Sound

As seen in his kind treatment of Adam and Eve, there are three ways in which God's grace is poured out: he clothes us, he protects us against ourselves, and he forgives us.

First, God clothes us with Christ (Galatians 3:26-27), calling us sons and daughters. Luke 15 is a beautiful New Testament chapter revealing the heart of God while Genesis 3 is a beautiful Old Testament one with the same message.

Next, now that we have experiential knowledge of sin, God keeps danger at arms' length, protecting us against ourselves. How often he has protected us from ourselves—our own worst enemy!

Finally, he forgives us. Sin does have certain consequences, but no record is kept. Redemption is full. Amazing grace! This is the heart of God, a Father who dares to forgive!

Notes

1. Grace has been defined by the acronym God's Riches At Christ's Expense.

2. The familiar hymn "Amazing Grace" has a not so familiar history. *"John Newton, Clerk, once an infidel and libertine, a servant of slaves in Africa, was by the rich mercy of our Lord and Saviour, Jesus Christ preserved, restored, pardoned, and appointed to preach the faith he had so long laboured to destroy near sixteen years at Olney in Bucks and... years in this Church..."* This epitaph was written by the very hand of the sailor it describes and at whose grave site it stands. Captain John Newton, a sailor from 1730-1748, had been involved in prodigal and profligate living, profiting personally from his role in the slave trade. He came to his senses during a vicious storm, reminded of the many Bible texts he had learned at the knee of his mother, who passed away when he was only seven. (Adapted from Lindsay L. Terry, *Devotionals from Famous Hymn Stories,* Grand Rapids: Baker, 1974.)

3. There is a word play here. To convey it fully in English, we would have to select some name like "Livia." Suggested by Daniel Lys, *Le jeu des mots dans l'Ancien Testament,* Revue Reformée 27 (1976), 105.

4. Creatures with earthly faces, occasionally mentioned in the Bible. Singular: *cherub,* plural: *cherubim.* They frequently serve in the capacity of guardian spirits.

The question arises, are these creatures *real?* They are not classed with the angels, who in Scripture are clearly created beings. Hundreds of ancient sculptures of cherubim have survived: you see them in the great museums of the world, like the British Museum in London and the Louvre in Paris. Cherubim were an invention borrowed from the ancient Near East, appropriated by God from pagan religion and "converted" for symbolic use in his Word, just as Paul borrowed from familiar pagan writers to help people understand Jesus' message.

5. Speaking of cavemen, Neanderthal man, first discovered around 150 years ago, were mistakenly considered a "missing link" between ape-like creatures and modern man (Homo Sapiens = "Wise Human"). After it was realised that Neanderthal Man was in fact *modern man*, Homo Sapiens was renamed *Homo Sapiens Sapiens* (do we detect some anthropological flattery here?). Neanderthals were accordingly renamed *Homo Sapiens Neanderthalensis.* (For more on Caveman, see Appendix D.)

6. In Judaeo-Christian speculation (shortly after the time of Christ), Adam and Eve, on leaving Eden, dwelled in the Cave of Treasures (found in the pseudepigraphal *Adam and Eve, Book I, 1:9*).

7. Grace is extended through God's call of Abram! There is yet hope for mankind—although the reader does wonder a bit after Genesis 11:9! Recall that the spiritual promises to Abram (12:3) were fulfilled in Christ, and Pentecost was *Babel in reverse.*

11

The First Homicide

Two Brothers

God, in his grace, gave mankind another chance. He gave family a chance. Ah, but we all know the grim end of this story. Well then, let us grab the rose, thorns and all, not fearing the pricks (of conscience) that may make us bleed. Because as long as we can still bleed, we are still alive.

> *4:1Adam lay with his wife Eve, and she became pregnant and gave birth to Cain. She said, "With the help of the LORD I have brought forth a man." 2Later she gave birth to his brother Abel.*
> *Now Abel kept flocks, and Cain worked the soil. 3In the course of time Cain brought some of the fruits of the soil as an offering to the LORD. 4But Abel brought fat portions from some of the firstborn of his flock. The LORD looked with favor on Abel and his offering, 5but on Cain and his offering he did not look with favor. So Cain was very angry, and his face was downcast.*

Cain and Abel are born, the most significant of Eve's offspring up to this point. Each presents sacrifices to God, yet Cain's are not presented according to God's will (Hebrews 11:4). It is evident from the text that Cain's "sacrifice" was a sacrifice in name only. He approached God in a pagan way: attempting to use God, instead of willing to be used by God. He is looking for credit. He feels that his religious acts ought to earn him something. And all they earn is a challenge.

The Lord challenges Cain's heart. We all need people in our lives who will challenge us when our level of sacrifice is slipping! However, Cain's reaction is one of extreme emotion-alism. Rather than take responsibility and repent, he prefers to wallow in self-pity.

> [6]Then the LORD said to Cain, "Why are you angry? Why is your face downcast? [7]If you do what is right, will you not be accepted? But if you do not do what is right, sin is crouching at your door; it desires to have you, but you must master it."

His unrighteousness is mirrored in his facial expression. The face says a lot (Proverbs 15:13; Isaiah 3:9; Mark 10:22; Psalm 34:5). Next time you are at church, look around at the eyes of other disciples. You will learn a lot about who is doing well spiritually!

Instead of mastering his selfish desires, Cain allows them to master him. What sins are "crouching at *your* door"? Be assured of this: Satan crouches, ready to pounce (1 Peter 5:8).[1]

Murder He Wrote

Cain, totally focused on himself, is easily overcome by sin. He schemes and murders his own brother. We too are "pushovers" for Satan when we are wrapped up in ourselves and "the things of men" (Matthew 16:23).

> [8]Now Cain said to his brother Abel, "Let's go out to the field." And while they were in the field, Cain attacked his brother Abel and killed him.
> [9]Then the LORD said to Cain, "Where is your brother Abel?"
> "I don't know," he replied. "Am I my brother's keeper?"

Cain asks the famous question, "Am I my brother's keeper?" God's (tacit) response: "Yes, you are." The people of God need to look after the people of God. Hebrews 3:12-14 could not be clearer! Our needs will never be fully met until we are totally devoted to the church, just as the early Christians were "devoted to the fellowship" (Acts 2:42).

Are you more like Cain (poor sacrifices, self-justification, feelings of jealousy and hatred) or Abel (pure sacrifices, hu-mility, love for God and your brother)?

The death of righteous Abel is a theme picked up in the New Testament and even applied to the death of Christ (Matthew 23:35; Hebrews 11:4, 12:24).

> [10]*The LORD said, "What have you done? Listen! Your brother's blood cries out to me from the ground. [11]Now you are under a curse and driven from the ground, which opened its mouth to receive your brother's blood from your hand. [12]When you work the ground, it will no longer yield its crops for you. You will be a restless wanderer on the earth."*

God opposes Cain; he is under a curse. Once again, the cycle of sin is repeated. Cain is banished to the land of Nod, where he will be a "restless wanderer," because only in God do our souls find rest (Psalm 62). What do we see in Cain's life? Not only separation from God, but also excuse-making. (Did he learn that from Mom and Dad?) Life becomes oppressive and he is restless, even paranoid (4:14).

To be sure, when we're involved in sin and self-pity, we'll never be at our best. But just as God knew Adam and Eve would need grace, so he knew Cain's life would take a sad turn. (Sin could be defined as a sad turn away from the will of God.) It is encouraging, however, that God gives Cain a fresh start.[2]

> [13]*Cain said to the LORD, "My punishment is more than I can bear. [14]Today you are driving me from the land, and I will be hidden from your presence; I will be a restless wanderer on the earth, and whoever finds me will kill me."*

The Fugitive

Cain flees. I remember as a seven-year-old getting into a fight with my brother, then five. We were quarreling over a toad, which had hidden itself in a woodpile. I struck him on the head with a piece of firewood, and he bled profusely. I still feel the heat of panic, the denial, and the fleeing, as I ran into the house and tried to hide from my parents and grandparents. And I remember the guilt. I remember *remembering* the story of Cain and Abel. I guess there was no confusion which character I was! My brother recovered quickly. But I would never let myself forget. Being a fugitive is no fun.

There was one huge difference between Cain and his father. Both had to leave after being confronted by God. But Cain was a fugitive, not just an exile. There is a difference. The words of Proverbs 28:17 seem to be fulfilled in Cain's life.[3]

A few more comments about the fugitive:

- We hear no word of regret from Cain, no plea for forgiveness.
- He cannot be rehabilitated, because he refuses to see the wrong he has done. As with many who go in and out of our prisons, with him there is little hope of true reform. The system is powerless to help those who do not want to help themselves.
- His dominant emotion is fear. He is restless. He has settled for a pathetic life, far from the fellowship his father offered, and is prisoner to his own "heart of darkness."
- He makes the Prodigal Son (Luke 15) look totally righteous in comparison!

> [15]But the LORD said to him, "Not so; if anyone kills Cain, he will suffer vengeance seven times over." Then the LORD put a mark on Cain so that no one who found him would kill him. [16]So Cain went out from the LORD's presence and lived in the land of Nod, east of Eden.

God's gracious treatment of the self-pitying fugitive is stunning! Protection is offered, including the mysterious mark of Cain—left somewhat to our imaginations to figure out. *Nod* is the word for "wandering." Interestingly, many names and places in this part of Genesis have symbolic significance.

So, who did Cain have in mind when he said, "Whoever finds me will kill me"? His father or mother? And whom did he marry (4:17) if there were now only three humans on the earth? And why build a city for such a small number of people?

Cain's Wife

Where did Cain find a wife? Was she a Cro-Magnon woman? A sister? Were Adam and Eve not the first humans? What's going on?

> *[17]Cain lay with his wife, and she became pregnant and gave birth to Enoch. Cain was then building a city, and he named it after his son Enoch.*

Some of the early Christians taught that Cain married a sister. The apocalyptic and pseudonymous 2 Enoch teaches that he married Luluwa, his twin sister but there may be more truth to this conjecture that one would think.[4] It seems possible that Cain was already married, and that his wife fled with him. At any rate, she is not an important character. (Not good at choosing a husband, either.)

Cain's building of a city is the beginning of urbanization[5]—and a whole host of ills to follow. We see also in 4:17 his concern about carrying on his name—to achieve immortality in the only way he could conceive: by forcing his memory on posterity.[6]

Adam's Family

Why should we think that Adam and Eve had only three children, Cain, Abel and Seth? If this is so, they disobeyed God's command to "be fruitful and multiply" until *after* the Fall. The problem with the "three sons theory" is Genesis 5:4, which says explicitly that they *did* have other children, both male and female. Isn't it reasonable to assume that Cain, Abel and Seth were rather the three most noteworthy of Adam's many children?

In my view Cain had to have married a relation. Wasn't that incest? you ask. Incest was not even defined until Leviticus

18. Even Abraham married his half-sister, Sarah. The genetic perils in marrying a cousin may not have existed at an earlier point in the history of mankind.

Doesn't the text imply a considerable population at the time of Cain's banishment? Yes, but considering Adam had more than one hundred years to produce children before Seth, there's no reason that Adam and Eve couldn't have procreated a population of many thousands.

> *[18]To Enoch was born Irad, and Irad was the father of Mehujael, and Mehujael was the father of Methushael, and Methushael was the father of Lamech.*

Cain's lineage begins. No one impressive yet. Not until Lamech. Warning: The impression isn't nice.

> *[19]Lamech married two women, one named Adah and the other Zillah.*

Lamech has the distinction of being the first polygamist in the Bible. Bigamy is not recommended, it's only recorded. (Incidentally, if the Old Testament shows us anything about polygamy, it shows that who practiced it paid the price! Consider, for example, the constant rivalry and bickering between Sarah and Hagar (Genesis 16), or Rachel and Leah (Genesis 29 and 30).

> *[20]Adah gave birth to Jabal; he was the father of those who live in tents and raise livestock. [21]His brother's name was Jubal; he was the father of all who play the harp and flute. [22]Zillah also had a son, Tubal-Cain, who forged all kinds of tools out of bronze and iron. Tubal-Cain's sister was Naamah.*

The line of Lamech raised livestock. They had time for music, and must have achieved some degree of refinement. His family also had a business: a forge. Gone are the simpler, olden days (the Stone Age[7]). We are now in the Early Bronze Age.

Song of the Sword

Next we come to the so-called "Song of the Sword." Lamech takes revenge, much in the spirit of his spiritual father Cain. And the punishment definitely did not fit the crime: death for personal injury. Lamech seems to have misunderstood God's righteous decree in 4:15. His "interpretation" of the word of God justified a heinous crime. We see in Lamech a totally self-centered individual:

> [23]*Lamech said to his wives,*
>
> *"Adah and Zillah, listen to me;*
> *wives of Lamech, hear my words.*
> *I have killed a man for wounding me,*
> *a young man for injuring me.*
> [24]*If Cain is avenged seven times,*
> *then Lamech seventy-seven times."*

Despite their similar psychological profile, Lamech was much more civilized than his ancestor Cain. He had technology; Lamech had the forge to produce the perfect weapon to deliver all seventy-seven blows. And he has the refinement of words—poetry—to express his brutality. How modern this sounds!

> [25]*Adam lay with his wife again, and she gave birth to a son and named him Seth, saying, "God has granted me another child in place of Abel, since Cain killed him."* [26]*Seth also had a son, and he named him Enosh.*
> *At that time men began to call on the name of the LORD.*

The lack of spirituality in the line of Cain was rampant. Their deeds and accomplishments were worldly: construction, music, metalwork and murder. Not that the first three are not useful, but there was no emphasis on God. What a contrast to the line of Seth! (Genesis 5:2-32).

Seth is "granted" in the place of Abel. At last Adam and Eve have a son again who makes spiritual sacrifices. It is only with the beginning of the godly line of Seth (Seth and his son Enosh) that mankind began to call on the name of the LORD. Throughout the generations of Cain, men and women had "missed their quiet times." They had "stopped going to church" altogether. "Their minds were on earthly things"! With Seth there was hope again.

Family Pain

Cain's murder of his brother was, in a real sense, the murder of Cain. He killed his own heart, seared his conscience, became alienated from all others and even alienated from himself. (It is beyond question that he also broke Eve's heart, and his father's.)

This homicide, technically a fratricide (slaying one's own brother), broke the heart of God. God would let his heart be broken again and again as mankind degenerated, as men and women created in the image of God followed the slippery path from Romans 1:21 to Romans 1:32. Soon God would have no choice.

Notes

1. An excellent book on preparing others for Satan's attacks is Mike Taliaferro's *The Lion Never Sleeps,* Woburn, Mass.: Discipleship Publications International, 1996.

2. Despite his criminal record, Cain was later able to get a wife and hold down a job in construction!

3. This chapter in Proverbs seems especially written for Cain and those who resemble him spiritually. See Proverbs 28:1, 5, 9, 13, 14, 17, 24 (in robbing his parents of their son), and above all, 26.

4. 2 Enoch I:74:5, II:1:6. Cain marries her after the stipulated period of mourning for Abel has run out. Abel also has a twin sister, Aklia (2 Enoch I:75:11), whom Seth marries (II:7:5).

5. "Permanent settlements begin to appear in the ancient Near East as early as the 9th and 8th millennia B.C. Jericho and Nahal Oren in Palestine, Mureybit in Syria, Çayönü in Anatolia and Ganj Dareh in Iran are probably the best known." Source: *The Times Atlas of the Bible,* 26, London: Times Books Ltd, 1987.

6. From an Israelite perspective naming the city after his son was a way of perpetuating his own memory.

7. More precisely, and probably more accurately with the biblical text in mind, the Neolithic Age.

12

Live Long and Prosper

Genealogy Splicing?

Genealogy has been defined as "tracing yourself back to people better than you are." I know my pedigree back a few generations—maybe you do, too. My forefathers sailed from Northern Europe to the American colonies in the seventeenth, eighteenth and nineteenth centuries. The Jacoby family proudly proclaims its English, Irish, German, Swedish and Finnish blood. Yes, we know there were ancestors before 1690, but for all intents and purposes we pretend they don't exist. Were these better people than us? Are we snobbishly flaunting our pedigree? God only knows.

The (Genesis) 5 & 10

For the ancient Jews, genealogies were far, far more important than for us today. Genesis dedicates two chapters (5 and 10) to the matter, and they deserve a few minutes of our time. Chapter 5 traces the descendants of Adam *in time*, reaching from Adam to Noah, while chapter 10 traces the descendants of Noah *in space*, reaching out from Ararat to the four corners of the land.

In a chapter about numbers the author hopes not to bore the reader. But fear not, we will not delve too deeply into matters genealogical. We'll take Paul's advice in 1 Timothy 1:4 and Titus 3:9 and not get too bogged down!

5:1a This is the written account of Adam's line.

Here is the second *toledoth* (generation) passage. Once again, the entire book of Genesis, a book about origins, is structured around ten generations.

1b When God created man, he made him in the likeness of God.
2He created them male and female and blessed them. And when they were created, he called them "man."

Genesis reminds us that man was created in the likeness of God, *male and female.* We are spiritually like God. The following genealogy is not just a list of names, as in the white pages of your telephone book; it reminds us of Luke 3, where a list of names bridges the gap between God and an historical figure who would save the world. There are parallels between Jesus and Noah.

The Line of Adam

3When Adam had lived 130 years, he had a son in his own likeness, in his own image; and he named him Seth. 4After Seth was born, Adam lived 800 years and had other sons and daughters.

Adam had Seth, "a son in his own likeness." This means not that Seth had Adam's ears and hair, but rather that (in the absence of Abel) Seth had the same spiritual commitment his father Adam had. Cain simply did not qualify.

Adam had other sons and daughters whose names we will never know. As we have suggested, some of these may have been born before the Fall.

800 years is a long time to have children, even after those born in his first 130 years. With modest assumptions and allowing relatives to intermarry, this span of time is more than sufficient to populate a planet, beginning with one couple![1]

5Altogether, Adam lived 930 years, and then he died.

Two Extremes

There are two extremes to avoid. The one is to fail to see the clear symbolism in Adam and his life, viewing him as just another historical individual. The other is to regard him as legend or myth, a story with a moral but nonhistorical. True, there is frequent shifting between the generic *Adam* (mankind) and individual *Adam* (the man) in Genesis 2:5-5:5. Unquestionably, the truth is in the middle. Despite his rather generic name, Adam is firmly rooted in history.

> *[6]When Seth had lived 105 years, he became the father of Enosh. [7]And after he became the father of Enosh, Seth lived 807 years and had other sons and daughters. [8]Altogether, Seth lived 912 years, and then he died.*

Observations

Seth became the "father" of Enosh.[2] The NIV footnotes in Genesis 5 and 10 often give "ancestor" as an alternative to "father," because in Hebrew thought, "father" can mean anything from "father" or "grandfather" to "distant ancestor," and "son" can mean "son," "grandson" or "a descendant of any kind."

Take Matthew 1:1: "A record of the genealogy of Jesus Christ the son of David, the son of Abraham." In fact many generations separate Jesus from David and David from Abraham. Two millennia are encompassed in three names! In 2 Chronicles 28:1 Ahaz's "father" is David, though in fact David is Ahaz's great, great, great, great, great, great, great grandfather! Moreover, men are said to rest with their "fathers" (2 Chronicles 16:13). It is obvious here that "fathers" are "ancestors" and "sons" are "descendants." Generally speaking, context determines whether the secondary meanings of "father" and "son" are being used.

With this in mind it seems doubtful that biblical genealogies can be interpreted as strictly as modern "family trees." They often skipped generations of less significant characters;

we would insist on identifying every link in the chain.[3] Only
the more prominent persons were mentioned—a principle
governing most genealogies in the Bible.

Another noteworthy observation: The "firstborn" in each
generation is male. The other sons and daughters are born "after" the significant son mentioned. In the case of Adam we know
that Seth was not, strictly speaking, the firstborn. This being
the case there is no reason to insist that the first-mentioned
males are the firstborn in any of the other generations, either.

The writer never tallies the ages of the patriarchs to give a
grand total. If he had, we might be entitled to do the same. It
is impossible to say how much time elapsed during the "ten"
generations of Genesis 5. The generations are not out of order, but clearly there are gaps.[4] But millennia ago the rules for
splicing together genealogies were radically different from rules
today.[5] In short, the genealogies served *theological* purposes
more than *chronological* purposes.

Someone Call Guinness!

> [21]*When Enoch had lived 65 years, he became the father of
> Methuselah. [22]And after he became the father of Methuselah, Enoch
> walked with God 300 years and had other sons and daughters.
> [23]Altogether, Enoch lived 365 years. [24]Enoch walked with God; then
> he was no more, because God took him away.*

> [25]*When Methuselah had lived 187 years, he became the father
> of Lamech. [26]And after he became the father of Lamech, Methuselah
> lived 782 years and had other sons and daughters. [27]Altogether,
> Methuselah lived 969 years, and then he died.*

Two intriguing characters from the genealogy are worthy
of special mention: Enoch, who did not die (but was "translated" to heaven)[6] and Methuselah, who at the ripe old age of
969 years, was the oldest man in history (5:27).

> [28]*When Lamech had lived 182 years, he had a son. [29]He named
> him Noah and said, "He will comfort us in the labor and painful*

toil of our hands caused by the ground the LORD has cursed." ³⁰After Noah was born, Lamech lived 595 years and had other sons and daughters. ³¹Altogether, Lamech lived 777 years, and then he died. ³²After Noah was 500 years old, he became the father of Shem, Ham and Japheth.

This portion of the genealogy brings us the rest of the way to Noah's generation. Noah, walking in the spirit of Abel and Enoch, is a righteous man living in an unrighteous age.

Long Life

What about the staggeringly high ages in Genesis 5? It isn't too difficult imagining a person today living to 150 or even 200 (a number of people in modern times have lived longer than 120 years). But what about 700, 800 or 900 years?[7] When I first read the Bible as a child, I guessed that their years must have been calculated on a different basis. I thought perhaps these were "lunar years," and so I divided all the ages by 12. The oldest men then lived to around 80, which seemed reasonable enough. But then Adam becomes Seth's father at age 13, which I could not bring myself to believe, while Kenan becomes the father of Mahalalel at the tender age of 6 years![8]

Others have proposed the idea that the patriarchs are actually tribes. But this would mean that the whole "tribe" of Enoch was whisked up to heaven (5:24).

Still others have suggested that long, long ago years may have been shorter than at the present day. But in fact the year was longer in ancient times. The year is losing 0.000015 seconds per day per year due to the slowing of the rotation of the earth. That would mean, if anything, that the ancients lived even longer (relative to our year) than Genesis says!

So what about the life spans? Did Adam live to be 930 years old? Yes, according to the Bible, and before plummeting longevity made this a virtual impossibility. Most likely (1) the men in question did reach the ages the Bible says (calculated in the solar years we are familiar with), because (2) conditions were different at that time. There is probably a bacteriological explanation. The curse on mankind seems to have lowered his life expectancy, as we see a tapering off of human ages through the book of Genesis.

What If You Lived 1000 Years?

Would living 1000 years radically affect your happiness? The productivity of your life? Would quantity somehow manage to outweigh and triumph over quality?

Suppose you lived to the ripe age of 95. I doubt you are banking on it! One of the most unusual surveys ever was a poll of people over 95. They were asked: If you could live your life over again, what would you do differently? These were the top three responses:

1. I would reflect more.
2. I would risk more.
3. I would do more things that would live on after I'm dead.

The unexamined life is not worth living, someone has said. Even if Christians who rush through life without taking time to ponder, to reflect, to plan and to communicate with their loved ones have the first fruit of the Spirit (love), they are surely missing most of the remaining eight! My wife saw a T-shirt the other day that said, "At 200 m.p.h., you don't have many friends." We laughed because I tend to rush through life, when often what is needed is a quiet afternoon with the family.

First, we are in God's family. God expects us to walk with him, not rush around like decapitated chickens. There must be some degree of peace and tranquillity if we are to reflect on the few days of our life on earth (Ecclesiastes 5:20).

Life Spans in Antiquity

It is widely thought that people in biblical times did not live as long as we do today. In fact the evidence suggests that many men and women lived well into their 70s and 80s. Psalm 90:10 speaks of a life span of seventy or eighty. This was around 1000 B.C. In New Testament times widows were not allowed to be enrolled unless they were over 60 (1 Timothy 5:9). Now you must admit that this policy would be cruel if first-century Israelites usually died in their 50s! In fact average longevity is a function of health and hygiene, diet, war, hardship and a host of other factors that vary from generation to generation.[9] Britons in the middle ages do not seem to have lived as long as Jews in the time of Christ.

It is a blatant demonstration of ignorance to affirm that in biblical times people died young. For all the medical and technological progress our century has seen, we have stretched human longevity very little indeed.

Second, we must not be "people-pleasers." Neutrality is no virtue! Someone has said, "The hottest places in hell are reserved for those who, in time to moral crisis, strove to preserve their neutrality." Do you take risks in the goals you set? In the evangelistic arena, for example? Are you bold in sharing your faith with the lost and following up with them? Taking risks is a mark of the true disciple. I like the way Teddy Roosevelt put it in 1899:

Far better it is to dare mighty things, to win glorious triumphs though checkered by failure, than to rank with those poor spirits who neither enjoy nor suffer much because they live in the gray twilight that knows neither victory nor defeat.

Third, we have an eternal purpose. Our mission is to reproduce the character of Christ in as many people as we can before we exit the stage of life. To reproduce that character—to bear the fruit of the Spirit—in our own lives, in our children, in those we have led to Christ, and in disciples whom we are able to influence and lead to be better disciples. Remember, Jesus died in his 30s. His public ministry lasted only three years. What he was able to achieve—well, the impact of that one man's life is infinite!

Disciples should and do pack more into a few years than those in the world do in a lifetime—more into one lifetime than those in the world could ever pack into 1000 years.

Conclusion

The line of Seth, stretching from 5:3 to 5:32, was godly. Men called on the name of the Lord (4:26). Many heroes in the faith are found in the ten-generation genealogy, most notably Enoch and Noah. This state of affairs—godliness and longevity to go with it—was not to last. Next we'll study the Flood, and see what happens when man turns away from his Creator on a massive scale.

To sum up, the genealogies are important because they (1) show the organic unity of the human race, (2) reveal the effects of righteousness and unrighteousness alike on the generations that follow, and (3) trace the ancestry that leads ultimately to Christ. As we have seen, genealogies are spliced together much more from theological motivations than from a determination to meticulously track each generation.

Finally, the accounts of great longevity should probably be taken at face value. Most important, in man's long trek through time and eternity, to live long in itself is nothing special, not if we don't prosper. And that is impossible if we fail to take time to gaze upon the very face of God.

Notes

1. One couple could have easily spawned a population of over 100 million in 400 years if there were only two children or grandchildren born every 16 years: that is, they doubled 6 times in a century.

2. Interestingly, *Enosh* is the usual Aramaic word for "man."

3. Omissions are common—a fact overlooked by Ussher when he laid the ages end to end to work out the creation date. Several factors should make us wary of using Genesis 5 for chronological purposes:

- Gaps are found in both OT and NT genealogical documents. 1 Chronicles 1:24 fails to mention *Cainan,* who is recorded in Luke 3:36. Going the other direction, after Matthew 1:8 the kings *Ahaziah, Joash* and *Amaziah* should be listed, but they are not.
- The number of generations is exactly *ten.* Remembering the author's fondness for *tens* (the generational structure of Genesis) we have reason to suspect a stylized genealogy.
- The firstborn is a male, in all ten successive generations. The odds against this are a whopping 1,000 to one! (2^{10}-1:1 @ 1000:1). Each patriarch had female offspring as well (5:4, 7, 10, 13, 16, 19, 22, 26, 30). It seems dubious we are to understand God played with chromosomes to guarantee each first child was male; it seems more likely that the genealogies are structured around *ancestral* precedence, not necessarily *biological* precedence.
- Modern translators recognize the frequent equivalence of *father* with *ancestor.* Their translations reflect this understanding more and more with each new version.

By the way, if Genesis 5 is mathematically precise and all-inclusive, Methuselah died in the year of the Flood, his son Lamech 5 years earlier. No one in Genesis 5 from the godly line of Seth drowned in the Flood.

4. "The most instructive lesson of all can be gleaned from Kohath's descent into Egypt (Genesis 46:6-11) some 430 years (Exodus 12:40) before the exodus. Now if Moses (one in Kohath's line) was 80 years old at the time of the exodus (Exodus 7:7), and no gaps…are understood…then the 'grandfather' of Moses had in Moses' lifetime 8,600 descendants. Amazing as that might seem, here is the real shocker: 2,750 of those 8,600 descendants were males between the ages of 30 and 50 (Numbers 3:19, 27, 28, 34; 4:36)! It is difficult to believe that the writers of Scripture were that naïve." (Source: Walter Kaiser, *More Hard Sayings of the Old Testament,* 23, Downers Grove: IVP, 1992). Kaiser is giving one of several proofs that we cannot and must not treat the genealogy of Genesis 5 as we might a modern genealogy.

5. It has been suggested (Archer, *A Survey of Old Testament Introduction,* [Chicago: Moody Press, 1964, 1974] p.198) that "the names in Genesis 5 represent an individual and his line by primogeniture—thus [we come] out to a grand total of 8,227 years between the birth of Adam and the flood. For example…this really means that Adam and his direct line were at the head of affairs for 930 years.… One difficulty with this theory, however, is that Seth is the oldest surviving son of Adam to be mentioned, apart from the exiled Cain, and it is difficult to imagine by what other son Adam's direct line would have descended before the allegedly collateral line of Seth took over."

6. Enoch was greatly venerated in Jewish tradition, two apocryphal works being ascribed to him.

7. Incidentally, the ages given in the Mesopotamian genealogies are much higher, running into the tens of thousands of years.

8. Of course we could postulate another miracle (on the short end of the longevity scale) to allow reproduction at such a young age. In general, when you need a second miracle to justify your theory about how a miracle happened, you are barking up the wrong tree.

9. In many parts of the world today the average life span is artificially depressed through institutionalised selfishness. Civil war, poor agricultural planning, the drug problem and other social ills keep the life spans in some countries low (less than 50 years), while other countries enjoy an average life span of 75 or 80.

13

Water Fall

The Flood and the Heart of God

World population in the time of Noah was skyrocketing.[1] In our own day population is fast approaching the six billion mark. Often through history, a population boom accompanies a decline in the quality of human life, particularly in the moral and ethical arena. Genesis 6 shows the quantity of human beings increasing as the quality of being human decreases. This does not mean you should move from your city to a small town. It does mean you cannot afford to ignore the lessons of history, especially in the period leading up to the Flood.[2]

> *6:1When men began to increase in number on the earth and daughters were born to them, 2the sons of God saw that the daughters of men were beautiful, and they married any of them they chose. 3Then the Lord said, "My Spirit will not contend with man forever, for he is mortal; his days will be a hundred and twenty years."*
>
> *4The Nephilim were on the earth in those days—and also afterward—when the sons of God went to the daughters of men and had children by them. They were the heroes of old, men of renown.*
>
> *5The Lord saw how great man's wickedness on the earth had become, and that every inclination of the thoughts of his heart was only evil all the time.*

Factors Leading up to the Flood

What were some of the causes of the Flood? Three factors are identified in the text.

Unspiritual marriages contributed, according to 6:2. The "sons of God" (see commentary below) were marrying for lust, not love. On what basis are you, as a single person, attracted to a man or woman? If you are married, which qualities do you value most in your spouse: physical or spiritual? Selfish and worldly decisions in the realm of dating and marriage can trigger catastrophe—just as in Noah's time!

Violence was another cause (6:11). In Noah's day, decadence and brutality marked a society in rebellion against God. In our own day, a quick look at the TV or a visit to the cinema will remind you that times have not changed all that much. Our days are becoming more and more like Noah's, and like the days of Roman society at the time of Jesus.[3] Our society is currently undergoing moral desensitization and moral disintegration on a colossal scale.

A third factor was *a deep and evil twist in the human character* (6:5). Things had been so bad for so long, and people were so apathetic toward the state of things, that the race became virtually beyond redemption.

Mixed Marriages

But who are these "sons of God" who married the "daughters of men"? While it may not be possible to give a conclusive answer, there are three theories which deserve some consideration.

Angels

"Sons of God" are angels. This is the most common view. "Sons of God" very often means "angels" in the Old Testament,[4] but fallen angels (demonic spirits) are never called "sons of God" in the Bible. Next, Matthew 22:30 creates serious problems for this interpretation, as Jesus states explicitly that angels do not marry. Besides, if they are the chief culprits, why did God not flood heaven? The traditional view may well have more kinship with mythology than mainstream theology. (By the way, Jesus doesn't say we become angels when we die; he says we become *like* the angels.) This view, however, does have the support of the pseudepigraphal *1 Enoch*, which Jude twice cites.[5] Does this mean, however, that Jude endorses everything in 1 Enoch?[6] No, because biblical writers often quote other sources and make use of them, without believing them to be inspired.[7]

Political Leaders

The second theory posits that the "sons of God" are political leaders. Psalm 82:6-7 (see John 10:34) lends support to this understanding. If this is correct, the passage is a comment on decadence among the leaders of the people. Their influence would have hastened the moral decay leading to the Flood. The corruption of political leaders does seem likely, and princes in the ancient Near East often claimed divine status, using the title "son of God." Moreover, they acquired vast harems of primary and secondary wives (concubines). Solomon's example is pertinent. The Aramaic targums (commentaries on the Torah) translated "sons of God" as "sons of nobles." Furthermore, the word for God, *elohim,* is translated "judges" in Exodus 21:6 and is parallel to the word "ruler" in Psalm 82:1, 6-7. Nimrod (10:8) is one such warrior (*gibbor* in Hebrew—the same word used in 6:4), and he is also a political leader (10:10).

Descendants of Seth

Last, the "sons of God" could have been the descendants of Seth.[8] In this theory the "daughters of men" represent the line of Cain, into which the line of Seth married. When even the righteous (Seth's line) are marrying for lust, the world is in a bad state! Though this interpretation initially seems forced, it fits with the flow of Genesis 4-6, connecting Cain with the Flood. One difficulty is the unusual use of the term "daughters of men." The Hebrew word man is *adam,* the very same word used a few lines earlier in 6:1. If this view is correct, the transition is abrupt, indeed, and unexplained.

Which View Is Right?

In my opinion, the second of these views dwarfs the others. We may have a hard time making our minds up because the term "sons of God" is almost completely unfamiliar to our age except as an epithet for Jesus Christ. You must decide for yourself which seems most logical. However you interpret the passage, it needs to fit into the broader context of Genesis 4-11.[9]

Through a Glass Clearly

> [6]*The LORD was grieved that he had made man on the earth, and his heart was filled with pain.* [7]*So the LORD said, "I will wipe mankind, whom I have created, from the face of the earth—men and animals, and creatures that move along the ground, and birds of the air— for I am grieved that I have made them."*

In 6:3 and 6:6 we have a direct window into the heart of God: God's Spirit can be grieved. God is emotional; he can be hurt.[10] The ultimate proof of this is Calvary. The "Passion" wasn't just the suffering of Jesus, Son of Man and Son of God; it was the suffering of God himself. God doesn't have to put up with rebellious children indefinitely. (Isn't it amazing that the Immortal puts up with us mortals at all?) There's a limit. One day God will intervene; the opportunity for repentance will be past. In the Flood we look through a window clearly into the kindness and sternness of God (Romans 11:22).

The 120 years is not a maximum set on human longevity.[11] It was the length of time remaining before, in one act of judgment, God would purge the earth and begin anew.

Giants?

Who are the "Nephilim" of 6:4? Are they a nonhuman race of giants?[12] Did these "mutants" survive the Flood, reappearing in Canaan as the "Anakites"?[13] Can angels procreate, with human assistance?

To begin with, it is highly doubtful that anyone would have escaped the judgment of God in the great deluge. The Nephilim were destroyed—yet they "came back." Since the word *Nephilim* literally means "fallen ones," the term speaks of moral character. They were "heroes," in the words of the writer. Every generation has its rowdy ones, its rebellious spiritual hooligans who wreak havoc wherever they go. In context the term seems to apply to those men described in Genesis 4 as bent on personal gain, revenge, lust—in short, the physical and spiritual descendants of Cain.

The verse says that they were on the earth "in those days—and also afterward"! So *how* did they come back? Were they reincarnated? Did they hold their breath for forty days during the worst of the flood? Or did they not rather "come back" because humans still carried the deadly sin virus which re-emerges in every human heart and every generation of mankind?

In 6:5 God speaks of the inclinations of the human heart. This is no proof-text for original sin![14] A tendency is one thing, actual sin is quite another. The doctrine of original sin asserts that we are born damned, guilty of Adam's sin. Certainly we are thoroughly marinated in our sinful surroundings. The signs are visible even from childhood (Proverbs 22:15). Genesis 6:5 says bluntly that the inclination of the human heart was evil all the time: a description of selfishness, apathy and godlessness on a massive scale. God is deeply grieved by the sin of his prodigal sons and daughters (6:6).

> [8]*But Noah found favor in the eyes of the* LORD.

> [9]*This is the account of Noah.*

> *Noah was a righteous man, blameless among the people of his time, and he walked with God.* [10]*Noah had three sons: Shem, Ham and Japheth.*

Enter Noah

Enter Noah, at the third *toledoth* passage. Noah, from the line of Seth, is "righteous and blameless" (6:9). He did not participate in the "flood of dissipation" (1 Peter 4:4) which characterized his generation. He "walked with God"; his relationship with God was truly his first love.

Exactly what does it mean to be righteous or blameless? "Blamelessness" does *not* mean perfection. Noah's sin recorded in Genesis 9 should be enough to dispel the notion that we are saved by perfectly keeping God's law. What it does mean is overlooked in our modern religious world: actively taking a stand to make a difference in the world. God knew Noah's heart—so different from the hearts of his contemporaries—and chose him to construct a vessel for the salvation of the remnant.

> [11]*Now the earth was corrupt in God's sight and was full of violence.* [12]*God saw how corrupt the earth had become, for all the people on earth had corrupted their ways.* [13]*So God said to Noah, "I am going to put an end to all people, for the earth is filled with violence because of them. I am surely going to destroy both them and the earth."*

Mankind had abused the gift of free will, voluntarily becoming corrupt. God therefore decreed destruction on the earth. Peter reminds us that in the same way God will destroy the earth next time by fire (2 Peter 3:3-7). The most important priority for you and me is to be ready for Judgment Day.

The flood to come would be totally destructive. I remember well our drive through a city only a few days earlier destroyed by flood: Rapid City, South Dakota, 1972. The immeasurable force of water smashed wood, twisted metal, flattened everything! It was declared a federal disaster area. I'd had no idea a flood could be so powerful.

Peter parallels the Flood to the waters of baptism (1 Peter 3:21). As much as the water annihilated the disobedient, it saved the obedient. Just as the waters lifted up the ark above the decay and destruction of the world, so the water of baptism lifts us up, through the resurrection, and cleanly separates us from a world under the judgment of God.[15]

> [14] "So make yourself an ark of cypress wood; make rooms in it and coat it with pitch inside and out. [15] This is how you are to build it: The ark is to be 450 feet long, 75 feet wide and 45 feet high. [16] Make a roof for it and finish the ark to within 18 inches of the top. Put a door in the side of the ark and make lower, middle and upper decks."

The Ark

The ark was indeed massive, with a capacity over 1.5 million cubic feet! Unlike the Near Eastern mythological accounts in which the ark is pictured as a three-tiered cube, the biblical ship had the perfect dimensions suitable for an ocean-going vessel! How did the Hebrews get it right while the Babylonians did not, considering neither were seafaring peoples, unless God really did speak to Noah and the Bible is the word of God? While the Bible is not a science textbook, when it does touch on matters scientific, you can count on it to get it right.

As for the sheer capacity of the ark, it was huge. There would have been no problem at all accommodating a gargantuan number of creatures on board. Whether cypress wood, gopher wood or hickory bark, the Hebrew word for the material is obscure. Many parts of the Middle East were heavily forested in Noah's day—no shortage of wood! So, choose the word for the wood that rhymes best in the song you are singing![16]

In Wrath, Remember Mercy

In the Flood we see not only God's wrath, but also his grace. The LORD was not obligated to save Noah any more than he had been obligated to give Adam a second chance, or to snatch Lot out of the cesspool of Sodom and Gomorrah (Genesis 19). The God we serve is a *good* God! Even in wrath he remembers mercy (Habakkuk 3:2). His kindness extends to the entire family of Noah.

> *[17]"I am going to bring floodwaters on the earth to destroy all life under the heavens, every creature that has the breath of life in it. Everything on earth will perish. [18]But I will establish my covenant with you, and you will enter the ark - you and your sons and your wife and your sons' wives with you. [19]You are to bring into the ark two of all living creatures, male and female, to keep them alive with you. [20]Two of every kind of bird, of every kind of animal and of every kind of creature that moves along the ground will come to you to be kept alive. [21]You are to take every kind of food that is to be eaten and store it away as food for you and for them."*
> *[22]Noah did everything just as God commanded him.*

Water Fall

The "water fall" is soon to begin, with a force to make Niagara look like drizzle by comparison! A flood to cleanse the pollution from the land, to "de-create" before re-creating all over again.

Noah was ready. He stood out sharply from his contemporaries because of his godliness and obedient attitude (6:22). He was willing to obey God's specific instructions. Are you?

Notes

1. No, there is no way to accurately estimate world population, since (1) there are no records (2) we cannot date the first humans and (3) we can only guess what put the brakes on population. A ballpark guess: 50,000 to 5,000,000.

2. The generations before the Flood are termed the "antediluvian age," and those living in that period are called "antediluvians," from the Latin *ante* ("before") and *diluvium* ("flood").

3. For an eye-opening overview of the early church's attitude toward the world, read David Berçot's works *Will The Real Heretics Please Stand Up*, 1989, *A Glimpse of Early Christian Life*, 1991, and *The Pilgrim Road: Insights from the Early Christians*, 1991, all Tyler, Texas: Scroll.

4. See Genesis 6:2, 6:4; Job 1:6, 2:1, 38:7 in the New American Standard Version (NASV).

5. Pseudepigrapha are writings (spuriously) attributed to men or women of faith long dead. Writing in their "name" and with their "authority," these "ghost" writers hoped their works would gain acceptance. From the Greek *pseudos* ("fraud") and *epigraphein* ("inscribe").

6. 1 Enoch dates from around 200 B.C., and claims in 6:1-7:6 that 200 angels descended to the earth, took wives, and fathered offspring whose height reached 300 cubits (450 feet)! For a thorough discussion of the issue of Jude's view of 1 Enoch's inspiration, see *Jude's Use of the Pseudepigrapha and its Sig-*

nificance for Biblical Theology by Greg Sterling, in *The Exegete,* July/August 1983 (2812 Harbour Drive, Antioch, CA 94509). By the way, there is nothing that explicitly says the sin in Jude 6 is the same as the sin in Jude 7—only that there is some parallel. Here the version of the Bible you are reading may influence your opinion.

7. As Paul did multiple times in his Areopagus speech (Acts 17:22-31).

8. This view was championed by Julius Africanus (170-240 A.D.) and Augustine of Hippo (354-430 A.D.).

9. Sometimes it is better not to have a position on a part of the Bible than to try to hold a conviction weakly. Did the first readers of Genesis share our confusion? Probably not. But at a distance of three and a half millennia there are some features of the account likely to escape us!

10. In theological debate it is sometimes maintained that God does not feel because feeling is a space-time activity. Malachi 3:6 is incorrectly taken to prove God's impassability (his inability to suffer). Genesis 6 and a host of other passages prove otherwise.

11. A conclusion sometimes drawn from a cursory reading of the text. Quite a few persons lived past the age of 120 *after* the deluge. To name a few: Abraham (175), Sarah (127), Isaac (180), Jacob (147), Aaron (123), Jehoiada (130) and Job (160+).

12. In pagan mythology we often come across a race of giants, the offspring of man and gods or angels. For instance, Greeks had the Titans, the Norse the Frost Giants.

13. There are several individuals the Bible describes as tall, for example, Saul, the first king of Israel, who stood a head taller than anyone else (1 Samuel 9:2). Archaeologists have unearthed a number of skeletons from ancient Israel; few are taller than 5'2". At 6'2" Saul would have caused quite a sensation!

The most notorious giant in the Bible is "a champion named Goliath" (1 Samuel 17:4), who stood 9'4". But he is never described as a member of a different species. Most likely he had a severe gland problem! Giantism in our day has produced individuals nearing the 9' mark; there's no need to cast aspersions on the Scriptures. (If we take 5'2" as the average male height, Goliath towered more than 4' above the other warriors!)

Then there are a number of peoples described as unusually tall. First, there are the Anakites in Numbers 13:33 and Numbers 13:28. Yes, the Israelites felt like grasshoppers (obviously a figure of speech); but does Moses intend for us to believe they actually were giants? Or that their cities were supernaturally gigantic? (13:28).

Other tall peoples are the Rephaites (Zamzummites), mentioned in Deuteronomy 2:20. And the Emites in Deuteronomy 2:10. In 1 Chronicles 11:23 we read of a huge Egyptian. In Isaiah 18:2 the height of the Cushites is mentioned, as in Isaiah 18:7. Isaiah 45:14 mentions the tall Sabaeans, another African people of considerable stature. Rephaites, Emites, Cushites, Sabaeans— apparently these peoples were taller than the Israelites, yet this hardly qualifies them as a race of giants!

14. The doctrine of Original Sin was popularized around 400 A.D. by Augustine the ex-Manichee and leader at Hippo, North Africa. Augustine was seeking a rationale for the practice of infant baptism, which was becoming

widespread in the fifth century. He based his view on the Latin translation of
Romans 5:12, where the word *because* was rendered *in whom*. [Greek *eph ho*
(*because,* possibly *in whom*); Latin *in quo* (in whom).]

One verse clearly refuting this doctrine is Ezekiel 18:20. Another approach
is to show that Psalm 51:5 is metaphorical, by comparing it to 58:3, 22:9 and
71:6—none of which makes sense when taken *literally*. Most churches teach
the doctrine of original sin, which means that babies are born damned. Now
[to employ an American analogy] it's bad enough to come up to bat with two
strikes already against you, but quite another matter when you've struck out
before you've even swung the bat! This false doctrine not only makes God
unfair, but flies in the face of many, many scriptures.

15. The second century Christian writer Irenaeus compared the ark to the
church, in which only those truly saved would escape God's condemnation.

16. *Gopher wood,* occurring only once in the Old Testament.

Oddly enough, the ambiguity of the word "ark"—referring to the ark of
the covenant (the box containing the Decalogue) or Noah's ark (the ship)—is
common both to the English word and the Hebrew word *tevah.* To make
things worse, *tevah* is also the word used for the basket in which the baby
Moses floated!

300 cubits x 50 cubits x 30 cubits ≈ 30 x 5 x 3: the perfect dimensions for
a modern seafaring craft! Its dimensions are actual, not symbolic, as in the
New Jerusalem, a cube of 12,000 stadia (1400 miles) in each dimension. They
are neither literally hyperbolic nor exaggerated, but true measurements.

14

Water, Water Everywhere

From Cosmos Back to Chaos

The total destructive forces of nature are about to break loose. Whereas in Genesis 1 we saw God form cosmos (order) out of chaos (disorder), in Genesis 7 we are going to witness *creation in reverse*. This was essential if mankind was to have a fresh start. The primeval waters of chaos, once vanquished, will rise again to claim possession of the earth. In the words of the poet Coleridge, it was "water, water, everywhere"![1] It's no surprise that the fiery end of the world is paralleled with this first aquatic destruction (2 Peter 3:1-7).

But before God "de-creates" the world, he has to allow the breaking of his own heart. Sin and apathy don't just hurt us and others; they fill the heart of God with pain.

> *7:1The LORD then said to Noah, "Go into the ark, you and your whole family, because I have found you righteous in this generation. 2Take with you seven of every kind of clean animal, a male and its mate, and two of every unclean animal, a male and its mate, 3and also seven of every kind of bird, male and female, to keep their various kinds alive throughout the earth. 4Seven days from now I will send rain on the earth for forty days and forty nights, and I will wipe from the face of the earth every living creature I have made."*
>
> *5And Noah did all that the LORD commanded him.*

Noah the Unique

Noah, as we saw in the last chapter, was unique in his time; no one else took a stand for truth like him (7:5). Disciples are unique on the planet in taking a strong stand: not just for issues—like any modern crusader—but a stand for personal integrity, honesty and righteousness. Once again, Noah's obedience is thrown into high relief.

> *⁶Noah was six hundred years old when the floodwaters came on the earth. ⁷And Noah and his sons and his wife and his sons' wives entered the ark to escape the waters of the flood. ⁸Pairs of clean and unclean animals, of birds and of all creatures that move along the ground, ⁹male and female, came to Noah and entered the ark, as God had commanded Noah.*

The mention of clean and unclean animals refers not to their personal hygiene, but their acceptability under the Levitical food laws (Leviticus 11), a pointer to the authorship of Genesis early in the time of Israel.[2] More clean animals were needed than unclean: for consumption as well as for sacrifice (8:20).

> *¹⁰And after the seven days the floodwaters came on the earth.*
> *¹¹In the six hundredth year of Noah's life, on the seventeenth day of the second month—on that day all the springs of the great deep burst forth, and the floodgates of the heavens were opened.*

Floods Above and Below

The great deep is a water source under the earth, possibly underwater springs. Its springs burst forth, and its waters rise at the same time that the floodgates of heaven are pouring down rain. Water coming up from below and down from above, converging on one man and his family, lifted between heaven and earth in a wooden ark for the salvation of mankind. (Does this sound familiar to your New Testament ears?)

The animals return to obey Noah. God's original plan had man over the animals. When the first couple obeyed the snake, they disrupted that plan and harmony. Here it is restored.

God never, ever meant for us to serve, obey or worship animals (Romans 1:23). Sadly, many pagan religions today do just that. Their temples are full of images of creatures, instead of the Creator.

> *[12]And rain fell on the earth forty days and forty nights.*
>
> *[13]On that very day Noah and his sons, Shem, Ham and Japheth, together with his wife and the wives of his three sons, entered the ark. [14]They had with them every wild animal according to its kind, all livestock according to their kinds, every creature that moves along the ground according to its kind and every bird according to its kind, everything with wings. [15]Pairs of all creatures that have the breath of life in them came to Noah and entered the ark. [16]The animals going in were male and female of every living thing, as God had commanded Noah. Then the LORD shut him in.*

The Lord himself sealed the ark; presumably Noah could not do it himself.[3] Nor can we save ourselves by our own effort or ingenuity. In the same way, at conversion God personally "seals" us, his sons and daughters, with the Holy Spirit (2 Corinthians 1:22; Ephesians 1:13-14).

> *[17]For forty days the flood kept coming on the earth, and as the waters increased they lifted the ark high above the earth. [18]The waters rose and increased greatly on the earth, and the ark floated on the surface of the water. [19]They rose greatly on the earth, and all the high mountains under the entire heavens were covered. [20]The waters rose and covered the mountains to a depth of more than twenty feet.*

The flood was not just a Mesopotamian flood, as many theologians believe, because the quantity of water was huge. Imagine submerging the Alps, the Rockies, the Andes, the Mtumba Mountains, the Himalayas—and with water to spare.

> *[21]Every living thing that moved on the earth perished—birds, livestock, wild animals, all the creatures that swarm over the earth, and all mankind. [22]Everything on dry land that had the breath of life in its nostrils died. [23]Every living thing on the face of the earth was wiped out; men and animals and the creatures that move along*

the ground and the birds of the air were wiped from the earth. Only
Noah was left, and those with him in the ark.
    [24]*The waters flooded the earth for a hundred and fifty days.*

Yes, the Flood story is well-known in pop culture and
Sunday School teaching, but unfortunately, as many fallacies
as facts are proclaimed concerning it.

Noah the Preacher

Did Noah share his faith during the years he built the ark?
Can we imagine a man of faith not warning his fellows? 2 Peter
2:5 describes him as a "preacher of righteousness." That certainly implies that he was communicating truth to the people of
his day. 1 Peter 1:11 and 3:19 in combination have also been
understood by some to teach that the Spirit of Christ preached
through Noah.[4] We may speculate (and preach) about Noah's
awkward relationships with his neighbors, yet the details are
unclear. That he took an unpopular stand is hardly in doubt.

Evidence for a Universal Flood?

Can we "prove" Noah's flood? Is there archeological evidence? Can we dig down far enough and find a layer of sedi-
ment everywhere in the world—the same age and at the same
level? That would be helpful, but such evidence has not yet
come to light.

There are flood deposits nearly everywhere in the world,
but they vary greatly in their depth, thickness and age. All
that can be said is that there is no direct geological evidence
as such.

Hundreds of flood traditions have survived the world over,
from China to Polynesia to the Algonquin Indians of the eastern United States. Probably many of these stories are versions
of the story of Noah first heard from early Christian missionaries. The most historically conclusive accounts are those from
Mesopotamia, which prove beyond doubt that a cataclysmic
flood occurred many thousands of years ago.[5] Here are just a

Misconceptions About the Flood

1. The animals entered two by two. This is only partially true, since clean animals entered *seven pairs at a time,* unclean animals *two pairs at a time* (Genesis 7:2).
2. Before the Flood a "vapor canopy," in which the floodwater was contained, covered the earth.[6] The Bible teaches no such thing.
3. The flood lasted only 40 days. In fact 150 days is the official length (7:24), and Noah was unable to disembark for more than a year on account of the floodwaters (8:14, see 7:11). Forty days was only the period of intensive rain (7:17).
4. The ark alit on Mount Ararat. The Bible says it "came to rest on the mountains of Ararat" (8:4); the specific mountain is unnamed.
5. The flood story was borrowed from the Babylonians. Actually both the Genesis account and the Babylonian story recount the same event: the first historically, the second mythologically.[7]

few of the Flood stories from around the world, with the hero who was saved in a boat:[8]

Utnapishtim[9]	(Babylon)	Ziusudra	(Sumeria)
Deucalion	(Greece)	Manu	(India)
Fah-he	(China)	Nu-u	(Hawaii)
Tezpi	(Mexico)	Manabozho	(Algonquin)

8:1 But God remembered Noah and all the wild animals and the livestock that were with him in the ark, and he sent a wind over the earth, and the waters receded.... 4 and on the seventeenth day of the seventh month the ark came to rest on the mountains of Ararat.

Is it possible that we might one day locate the remains of Noah's Ark?[10] This is highly unlikely; beware claims of "satellite sightings" of the timbers from the original ship! These are no more reliable for building solid faith than the Shroud of Turin or the apparitions of Mary at Medugorje.

> *[14]By the twenty-seventh day of the second month [of the second year] the earth was completely dry.*
>
> *[5]Then God said to Noah, [16]"Come out of the ark, you and your wife and your sons and their wives. [17]Bring out every kind of living creature that is with you—the birds, the animals, and all the creatures that move along the ground—so they can multiply on the earth and be fruitful and increase in number upon it."*

Genesis 8:1 is the exact center of the Flood narrative, running from 6:9 to 9:17. It is the 39th verse; there are 38 verses before it and 38 verses after it. The narrative has a perfect symmetry—beyond the scope of this book—which shows how carefully the account has been composed. God "remembered Noah."[11]

> *[18]So Noah came out, together with his sons and his wife and his sons' wives. [19]All the animals and all the creatures that move along the ground and all the birds—everything that moves on the earth— came out of the ark, one kind after another.*
>
> *[20]Then Noah built an altar to the LORD and, taking some of all the clean animals and clean birds, he sacrificed burnt offerings on it. [21]The LORD smelled the pleasing aroma and said in his heart: "Never again will I curse the ground because of man, even though every inclination of his heart is evil from childhood. And never again will I destroy all living creatures, as I have done.*

Exit Stage Left

Eventually the ark alights on one of the mountains of Ararat, the waters recede, the ground dries up. After more than a year aboard the boat, the family of Noah[12] treads *terra firma* again. (Which would you take, a year aboard the Ark or the Mir Space Station?)

Sacrifices are presented (8:21),[13] God vows never to destroy the earth again (before the final curtain comes down on human history, of course), and agriculture resumes (8:22). At any rate, God makes a promise: never more to curse the ground, which has now received its second curse (counting 3:17).

In 8:21 God remarks that every inclination of the heart is evil from childhood. This is not *original sin,* but the Bible definitely does teach a "proclivity to sin," or a leaning toward sinful behavior. That is why the school of child psychology thought that says "Don't interfere with Johnny's behavior (i.e. Don't interrupt his tantrum!); he needs to express himself" is dead wrong. As parents we *need* to interfere, otherwise we will be discipling our children in the character of Cain.[14]

God then reiterates his promise never again to disrupt the cycles of nature and agriculture:

> [22] *"As long as the earth endures,*
> *seedtime and harvest,*
> *cold and heat,*
> *summer and winter,*
> *day and night will never cease."*

In other words, we do not need to brace ourselves for any global cataclysm. Being ready to meet God, however, is another issue entirely. Every book of the Bible aims to prepare us for that day.

Lessons, Lessons Everywhere!

The Flood account of Noah is more than a children's story. It is replete with lessons of a practical nature for you and me:

- Judgment is real; prepare for it well in advance. Noah spent many years preparing, and so must we.
- Salvation is real, too; it isn't just an idea, a feeling or a theory. Though realities beyond our everyday experience may occasionally be hard to visualize, they are real nonetheless.

Noah's "neighbors," and Noah himself, may have only faintly imagined what the Deluge would entail. But it came, in reality, with certainty and full force. This is not a game!

- Bring your family with you. You may be successful, like Noah, partially successful, like Lot, unsuccessful, like Samuel or apparently unsuccessful now only to be totally successful later, like Jesus.[15] But make every effort to get everyone "aboard." Have you taken a stand for Christ, in love, with your family members?

- Follow instructions; dare to obey the word of God, like Noah. His obedience is emphasized over and over again. To him details, faithfulness and reliability mattered. He knew the heart of God!

- Realize that the God we serve longs to forgive. In Christ, whenever we need grace (Hebrews 4:16, 7:25) we have the chance to become new creations ("re-created") in Jesus. "The old has gone, the new has come!" (2 Corinthians 5:17).

Notes

1. Samuel Taylor Coleridge (1772-1834), *The Ancient Mariner,* Pt. ii: "Water, water, every where/And all the boards did shrink/Water, water, every where/Not a drop to drink."

2. Even if it was written earlier than the formation of the nation (1146 B.C.), God worked his purposes so that the account was preserved to meet the needs of his covenant people millennia later.

3. It has been suggested that since the Ark was higher than Everest, 30,000 feet above sea level, it would have needed pressurization—just like modern jetliners flying at similar altitudes. God's "sealing" was his pressurizing of the Ark. Such wild suggestions are common among those who see the Bible as a science book. Moreover, the entire story of Noah and the Ark has a miraculous side to it. The question is not, What could God have done?, but What does the Bible clearly teach? The truth of Genesis remains intact regardless.

4. See my book *Life to the Full,* pp. 86-88 (Woburn, Mass.: Discipleship Publications International, 1995) for further discussion of this theme.

5. Now there are three, and only three, possibilities as to the extent of the Flood:
- No extent: The Flood is a myth concocted by the ancient Hebrews.
- Local extent: A local flood, probably Mesopotamian.
- Global extent: A universal deluge.

While the concocted myth view must naturally be rejected, Bible believers are divided over whether the flood was universal (the natural reading of Genesis 6-9) or local. Both views have problems and require a miracle to account for the voluminous amount of water as well as its recession in so short a time. The Bible often describes local events in universal language. For example, Genesis 41:57 says "all the countries" came to Egypt for relief during the famine. Are we to conclude that the ancient Mongol tribes journeyed to Northeast Africa? Or that the Mesoamericans crossed the Atlantic for food? 1 Kings 18:10 is another such passage. In the NT we must deal with Acts 2:5: Why are only 14 regions mentioned if pilgrims had come *literally* "from every nation under heaven"? Then there is Colossians 1:23, which is plainly being used metaphorically. After all, Acts and the letters do keep pretty good tabs on the spread of the gospel, informing us of new frontiers for evangelism and prayer.

If the local flood advocates are right and the flood struck Mesopotamia, that doesn't mean mankind could not have been wiped out. Even a local flood could have killed all men *if* everyone lived in the same part of the world.

The usual Hebrew word for earth or land, *'erets,* appears frequently in the flood narrative. The broader word *tebel,* meaning "the entire earth," is not used. This distinction is not conclusive, however, for local flood advocates.

Most Christians opt for the universal flood, since it is the most obvious reading. A local flood would explain why the passengers don't seem to include such creatures as kangaroos and walruses, as well as the lack of mention of an animal "dispersion" after their release from the boat (8:19). The local view makes better sense of the Table of Nations (see Chapter 10), which names only lands in the general area of the Middle East, and was clearly not intended to apply to the entire earth. Yet even the local view must explain 7:19, which requires more water than would be available in *any* flood—apart from a miracle. If only a supernatural process can cover mountains with water, "how much" miracle is required is a non-issue. This is a point for the universal view.

While we should be hesitant to concede too much to the critics, whose lives and doctrine are so confused already, it is not crystal clear from the biblical evidence which interpretation is correct. You must make your choice.

6. The "canopy" is a key idea in scientific creationism. The question they are trying to answer: What is the source of the water which flooded the earth? Assuming the Flood happened in the last 10 to 50,000 years, the present mountains were all in place. There is zero evidence that the present geological features of the earth were caused by the Flood! John Whitcomb's *The Genesis Flood,* the leading work of "Flood Geology," is disappointing. However, I do recommend this book as a way of becoming familiar with this kind of "science." For another presentation of the Canopy Theory see Isaac N. Vail's *Waters Above the Firmament,* Santa Barbara: Annular Publications, 1996.

Taking 7:19 literally, more than 5 miles of water is required on top of the present ocean levels, as Mt. Everest is between 29,028 and 29,100 feet high, or 5.5 miles.

Since the earth's diameter is 7926 miles, the radius (R_1) is approximately 3963 miles. This assumes the perfect sphericity of the earth; in fact, the earth bulges at the equator, and the Southern Hemisphere bulges more than the Northern, creating a slight pear shape! The volume of the additional amount of water (V_w) is the difference in the sizes of the volumes of the sphere created by the Flood and normal sphere of the earth. This may be expressed mathematically by

$$V_w = V_2 - V_1 = \quad \pi R_2^3 - \quad \pi R_1^3 = \quad \pi (R_2^3 - R_1^3) =$$

$$\pi (3968.5^3 - 3963^3) \approx 1,087,000,000 \text{ mi}^3$$

This is over a billion cubic miles. (Imagine a cube of water a 1000 miles x 1000 miles x 1000 miles!) That's an extra 3 to 4 times the amount of water in all the oceans (322,300,000 cubic miles), assuming underground water sources of floodwater (8:2) were relatively small. With this amount of water in the clouds, atmospheric pressure would approach 1000 p.s.i. Your whole body would experience a flattening sensation not unlike a steamroller driving over you! It would have been easier to live *through* the flood than before it! Then, once the waters had fallen from the sky, "decompression" would have caused us to suffer nitrogen narcosis—the "bends"! Not only that, but if it took 2.5 months for 20 feet of water to subside (8:6, 13-14), it would have taken more than 300 years for the entire 5.5 miles to subside! Worst of all for the scientific creationists, Psalm 148:4 says that the "waters [or floods] above the sky" are still there. The canopy theory, to sum up, simply doesn't "hold water"!

7. The Babylonian version is roughly parallel to the biblical account, including a god warning a man, the animals, the birds sent out on reconnaissance, the sacrifice after disembarking from the ark and several other features. At the same time there are many incorrect details; the Mesopotamian accounts, though of historical value, are clearly corrupted traditions about the original events which Genesis accurately records.

8. Other traditions include those of the tribesmen of Lake Caudie (the Sudan), the aborigines of the Andaman Islands (Bay of Bengal), the Battaks of Sumatra (Indonesia), the Kurnai of Australia, the ancient Celts of Wales, the Fijians, the Greenlanders, the Hottentots, and natives of Micronesia, Polynesia, New Zealand, Papua New Guinea and the New Hebrides.

9. Similar to another pre-Noachic figure, *Atrahasis*, hero of the Akkadian *Myth of Atrahasis*. In the Gilgamesh Epic, Tablet IX, Gilgamesh meets Utnapishtim, who, with his wife, had survived the flood, which is recounted in Tablet XI. Utnapishtim means *He found life*; Atrahasis means *Extra wise*. The name of the Sumerian Ziusudra means *Long life*.

10. As claimed in the pop-science book and docudrama *In Search of Noah's Ark*.

11. See also Genesis 9:15-16. The theme of *God's remembering* is perhaps strongest in Nehemiah (1:8, 5:19, 6:14, 13:14, 22, 29, 31).

12. Noah, his wife, his sons Ham, Shem and Japheth and their wives. There may also have been infants on the ark. Biblical numbers often exclude children, or women and children (e.g. Numbers 2:32; Matthew 14:21). Peter would have been aware of this (1 Peter 3:20), counting as *eight* the number of those [adults] saved through the Flood. Yet 10:1 implies any children born before the Flood were daughters, not sons.

13. In the pagan account, the gods buzz like flies around the sacrifices,

since they have been "starved" for food for some two weeks (the duration of the flood).

14. Proverbs gives a good deal of parenting advice, especially chapter 29 (verses 15, 17, 19, 21). For an excellent discussion of this matter see *The Call of the Wise* by G. Steve Kinnard (Woburn, Mass.: Discipleship Publications International, 1997).

15. Genesis 19:14, 26; 1 Samuel 8:1-3; Mark 3:20-21, 31-35, 6:1-6; Acts 1:14.

15

Terra Firma

Life After Waterworld

Do you ever feel like your life is in limbo? Maybe you just moved, or are about to move. Maybe you're between jobs. Maybe you're in a new church or have entered a new circle of friends. Maybe life is topsy-turvy: Did you just become a father or mother? Are the kids going through a very "demanding" phase? Maybe you are in some other transition, and you feel like you're drifting.

After more than a year of "drifting," Noah and his family must have been eager to get back to life as normal. "Waterworld" can be quite unsettling. Limbo tends to unnerve its residents.

The creation had been severely traumatized through the effects of sin, yet God in his wisdom and mercy had dared to "re-create" by sparing a remnant through whom he would repopulate the earth. Our final chapter devoted to Noah explores the issues raised by Genesis 9 and 10.

> *9:1Then God blessed Noah and his sons, saying to them, "Be fruitful and increase in number and fill the earth. 2The fear and dread of you will fall upon all the beasts of the earth and all the birds of the air, upon every creature that moves along the ground, and upon all the fish of the sea; they are given into your hands. 3Everything that lives and moves will be food for you. Just as I gave you the green plants, I now give you everything."*

After the Flood

God recommissions man to "be fruitful and multiply" (9:1), reminding Noah of what he most surely already knew. Do you complain when you are "reminded" of your mission—as though you had forgotten? (Maybe you had!) Often getting back to basics is the way to get life on an even keel again. Consider a few areas:

- Consistent times for prayer and Bible study. Does your schedule need revamping?
- Regular meal times for you and the family. The kids certainly need it, and so do you.
- Getting a grip on your personal discipline. Organize those papers; clean that apartment; get up with the alarm clock; be early for work, appointments, church. Are you always "cutting it close"?
- Being involved in the lives of unbelievers. There's nothing that will straighten our hearts out (when they get bent out of shape) as effectively as evangelism!

Green Eggs and Ham, Anyone?

Noah's relationship with the natural order is somehow changed. This passage apparently marks the transition from vegetarianism to meat eating (9:3-4). The religious doctrine of vegetarianism as proclaimed today, despite the insights and sound medical sense it often shows, finds no support in the Bible. (See also Mark 7:19.) Nowhere does the Bible teach that man became a meat-eater as a result of the curse in Genesis 3.[1] Under the first covenant, the Jews did have certain dietary restrictions, but now all foods are clean (Acts 10:15).

> [4]*"But you must not eat meat that has its lifeblood still in it.*
> [5a]*And for your lifeblood I will surely demand an accounting. I will demand an accounting from every animal."*

Blood

Why was consumption of blood forbidden?[2] First of all, it may be in part for hygienic reasons, since drinking blood is an unsanitary practice—though prevalent in the world of pagan religion, especially in antiquity. Second, drinking blood is a pagan practice, and God's people are called by God to distance themselves from paganism (Deuteronomy 12:4; 2 Corinthians 6:17-18). Third, drinking blood is an irreverent practice, since the blood is the means of atonement for sin, and to drink it would be to disrespect the sacrificial system God had instituted (Leviticus 17:11).

> [5b]*"And from each man, too, I will demand an accounting for the life of his fellow man.*
>> [6]*Whoever sheds the blood of man,*
>>> *by man shall his blood be shed;*
>> *for in the image of God*
>>> *has God made man."*

Notice that the Fall did not "erase" the image of God in man. Homicide is therefore not only a sin against the murder victim and his family, but a grave sin against the Creator, who had imparted his image to the murdered one.

Excursus: The Death Penalty

So special is human life, so seriously does God take murder, that capital punishment was instituted for homicide (9:6).[3] Under the old covenant it was mandated for other crimes as well, not to be discussed here, though a meaty footnote is provided.[4] Interestingly, the God of grace protected Cain from a death sentence after taking his brother's life (Genesis 4).

It was common biblical and rabbinical practice to accept monetary compensation in lieu of the specified penalty for a crime, except in cases of first degree murder (Numbers 35:31). In others words, the Old Testament law was more lenient in its application than in theory.

2 Samuel 12:5-6 (David's response to Nathan's parable after the murder of Uriah the Hittite) reflects the common Jewish practice of allowing compensation for damages. David says first "the man who did this deserves to die" (2 Samuel 12:5); then "he must pay...four times over" (verse 6). Once again, compensation was allowed for all crimes except murder. Legally speaking, however, David should have been executed for his adultery (Leviticus 20:10). That is why Nathan tells him, "The Lord has taken away your sin. You are not going to die" (2 Samuel 12:13). God can make exceptions to his laws, and this should serve as a warning to us not to be overly dogmatic.

Capital punishment is a topic on which true Christians may not see eye to eye. The issue is especially complex since, by its original stipulations, the death penalty was part of a penal system in a church-state, whereas under the new covenant, church and state are separate. A spirit of grace should be shown. Never make this issue or any other peripheral issue a "shibboleth" (Judges 12:6) for the purpose of establishing circles of fellowship. Because you might well be wrong. And if you were, who knows, you might change your mind in time—I certainly have!

Ultimately the issue will be legislated by your national government. At that point you have a responsibility to submit to the authorities, even where capital punishment is practiced (Romans 13:4).[5]

> [7] *"As for you, be fruitful and increase in number; multiply on the earth and increase upon it."*

Blue Skies, Rainbows and Wine

The biological great commission is reissued. Life must be protected, yet it must also be reproduced on the earth.

God now reestablishes his covenant. The Lord has always worked through a covenant, an agreement or contract between God and man.

> *⁸Then God said to Noah and to his sons with him: ⁹"I now establish my covenant with you and with your descendants after you ¹⁰and with every living creature that was with you—the birds, the livestock and all the wild animals, all those that came out of the ark with you—every living creature on earth. ¹¹I establish my covenant with you: Never again will all life be cut off by the waters of a flood; never again will there be a flood to destroy the earth."*
>
> *¹²And God said, "This is the sign of the covenant I am making between me and you and every living creature with you, a covenant for all generations to come: ¹³I have set my rainbow in the clouds, and it will be the sign of the covenant between me and the earth."*

God provides a visible sign of his covenant not to destroy the earth by flood: a rainbow.[6] Some scholars see the rainbow as a warrior's bow (a weapon) now pointed skyward, thus showing that God is no longer at war. But who was he at war with—sinners, or the earth? There was no "war." The Flood was a surgical procedure to morally sanitize the planet. Other scholars suggest that the rainbow (a cross-section of the firmament) was to assure the people that the dome of the firmament would no longer allow a cataclysmic flood.[7] Whatever its deeper meaning, the sign of the rainbow occurs frequently enough to be an excellent reminder of God's covenant faithfulness to the faithful.[8]

> *¹⁸The sons of Noah who came out of the ark were Shem, Ham and Japheth. (Ham was the father of Canaan.) ¹⁹These were the three sons of Noah, and from them came the people who were scattered over the earth.*
>
> *²⁰Noah, a man of the soil, proceeded to plant a vineyard. ²¹When he drank some of its wine, he became drunk and lay uncovered inside his tent. ²²Ham, the father of Canaan, saw his father's nakedness and told his two brothers outside. ²³But Shem and Japheth took a garment and laid it across their shoulders; then they walked in backward and covered their father's nakedness. Their faces were turned the other way so that they would not see their father's nakedness.*

Noah had been a farmer before the flood, and he now

Useful Verses on Alcohol

The following passages may "go against the grain" of our culture, but they are God's warnings to us, scattered throughout the Scriptures, for our health and happiness.[10]

Proverbs 20:1	Proverbs 23:29-35	Habakkuk 2:15
Luke 21:34	Romans 13:12-14	Romans 14:21
Galatians 5:21	Ephesians 5:18	1 Timothy 3:3
	1 Peter 4:3-4	

---

plants a vineyard. Unfortunately, he gets drunk on the wine he produces and lies uncovered in his tent. Enter Ham.

Noah's son Ham gazes on his father's nakedness in some perverse way and brings a curse on his family (9:25).[9] Shem and Japheth have more shame, and protect their father's honor. After Noah is sober, they tell him about Ham's shameful behavior.

What about you? Do you ever drink too much? One of the dangers of alcohol is the impairment of judgment, not just your ability to drive a car but your ability to make sensible decisions and conduct relationships in a selfless and godly manner. Drinking alcohol is not a sin, but it can so easily become one! Noah had too much wine. Don't be self-righteous! He was not an evil man; in Genesis 6 he was described as "blameless." No one—absolutely no one—is "above" falling into sin.

> [24]When Noah awoke from his wine and found out what his youngest son had done to him, [25]he said,

> "Cursed be Canaan!
>   The lowest of slaves

will he be to his brothers."
²⁶*He also said,*

"Blessed be the LORD, the God of Shem!
May Canaan be the slave of Shem.
²⁷*May God extend the territory of Japheth;*
may Japheth live in the tents of Shem,
and may Canaan be his slave."

The "Curse of Ham" in Context

The "curse of Ham," which landed on Canaan (the man), must be seen in historical context. It is meant to prove that the inhabitants of Canaan (the land), into which the Israelites in Moses' day are about to enter, do not deserve to live there.[11] As the reader, always ask, What would this have meant to those who first heard/read it? Otherwise we will fall into the trap of eisegesis instead of doing good exegesis.[12] Myriad false doctrines have been based on eisegesis, often with tragic consequences.

The "curse of Ham" has been the most repeated "biblical" racist argument in the history of Christendom.[13] Slaveholders, and even some missionaries, taught that Shem, Ham and Japheth represent the races of whites, blacks and Asians. Jesus was presumed white, though this is a fallacy since people in the Near East aren't white! Ham was black, so it is claimed. Genesis 9:18 says he was the ancestor of the Canaanites, whom God said to annihilate. This interpretation obviously encourages genocide, slavery and exploitation.

Excursus: The Curse of Ham and Racism

Prejudice is ugly, widespread, and knows no borders. Yet even more detestable is the use of biblical authority to justify racism. Through the centuries there have always been people who have used religion for selfish ends. Scriptures have been wrested from their context to support countless creeds of convenience and crass self-interest. And the wounded number in the millions, from victims of children's taunts to victims of "ethnic cleansing." They are found in every nation of the world, and, despite the common claim of professing Christians that they love their neighbors as themselves, little if anything is done.

1. *First false charge: Descendants of Ham are cursed today.* Noah cursed Canaan, Ham's son, for his perversity, which has continued in the line of Cain. Blacks, Native Americans and others are still under this curse, which explains their poverty and struggles. The visible mark of the curse is dark skin.

Refutation: To begin with, Ham had four sons:[14]

Cush:	Also a nation roughly corresponding to modern Sudan.
Mizraim:	Ancestor of peoples including Philistines. Means "Egypt."
Put:	More obscure group of peoples, probably North African.
Canaan:	Ancestor of morally degenerate Canaanite tribes.

The Hamitic peoples are explicitly said to be descendants of Ham, yes, but the curse applies specifically only to the Canaanites—a curse realized intensively during the Israelite conquest of Canaan. Once again, it wasn't Ham who was cursed, but his son, Canaan. So-called Christians using this passage to justify racism show an appalling prejudice as well as ignorance of the biblical text.

The "curse of Ham" is not a curse on Hamitic peoples, such as Egyptians, but a curse on one part of the Hamitic peoples who, oddly enough, weren't black at all! The curse became reality as the Canaanite nations sank deeper and deeper into apathy, immorality, godlessness—even into child sacrifice. Eventually God commissioned the Israelites to totally remove them from the land.

Incredibly, in racist societies through the centuries, religious bigots have preached that the curse on Ham was dark skin! Yet the Canaanites' pigmentation was probably no darker than Adam's, Mary's or Jesus'.

2. *Second false charge: "White supremacy."* Wasn't Adam a white man? Since "Adam" in Hebrew is the same word for both "mankind" and "red," and since blacks and other races don't have pinkish skin, nonwhites do not classify as human beings. They may belong to the animal kingdom, but they have no soul. It is unreasonable to claim that nonwhites have equal rights with whites. "Edom," another name for Esau and the nation of which he is ancestor, means "red, ruddy," and this is the same word as that for "man."

Refutation: We're dealing with two different words in Hebrew. They have the same consonants (', *d*, *m*) but different vowels (*a, a* vs. *a, o*), and may be related etymologically, but they're listed *separately* in the Hebrew lexicon: (' is the consonant *aleph*.) The confusion arises because Hebrew words are normally written *without* vowels.

> 'adham = man, mankind; 'adhamah = ground, from
> which man was made.
> 'adhom = red, as the skin color of Esau. From an ob-
> solete word for "tawny."

As an illustration of our unfamiliarity with Hebrew, take the English words *fever* and *favor.* The consonants are the same (*f, v, r*), but the vowels are different (*e, e* vs. *a, o*). Are the two words related? No, but if you took out the vowels (Hebrew was written without vowels) they could be confused. So it is with the *adham/adhom* confusion.

Along the lines of the thinking above, some people reason that since God created man "in his image," and yet we see human beings of many different physical appearances, only one race was created in the image of God. Colored peoples (Indian, Mongolian, Negro, Polynesian, Melanesian) are thus not truly created in God's image.

The image of God is a *spiritual* image, not a physical one. His spiritual image includes such aspects as spirituality, moral capacity, forgiveness, and abstract reasoning. God is beyond our concept of physical "image" because he is beyond our three-dimensional universe. Moreover, Jesus, being Semitic, would fail to qualify, since Semites aren't a white race. (This also contradicts Colossians 1:15, which says Jesus is the image of the invisible God.)

Summary: Religious Racism. The Bible in no way encourages or condones racism in any form. 1 John 4:20 makes it unequivocally clear that those involved in hatred in any form will not go to heaven. Still, the "Curse of Ham" argument dies slowly.[15] Before we leave this excursus, some questions for you and me:

- How many good friends do you have from your own ethnic background?
- How many good friends do you have from a *different* ethnic background?
- Would you feel comfortable in a "segregated" church? Do you think Jesus would?
- Do you reach out to people only of your own race?
- Do you feel any *class* of people is "beyond redemption," education or hope?
- How much does it bother you when you see groups of people being oppressed or exploited on the basis of their ethnic background?
- How many Bible verses do you know that show the heart of God about racism? That speak of his love for all nations?

The Lord has made it crystal clear that there is no room for racism among his children. To be godly we must dare to speak out against racism in all of it various ugly and disgusting forms.[16]

Multiplying on the Earth

> [28]*After the flood Noah lived 350 years.* [29]*Altogether, Noah lived 950 years, and then he died.*

Like Adam and Methuselah, Noah lived to an extremely ripe old age. The Bible says that he lived 950 years, "and then he died." (What else do you do after 950 years?) We have learned much from this great man of faith. As Hebrews 11:7 reads,

> *By faith Noah, when warned about things not yet seen, in holy fear built an ark to save his family. By his faith he condemned the world and became heir of the righteousness that comes by faith.*

From his offspring—Shem, Ham and Japheth[17]—the ancient world was repopulated.

> [10:1]*This is the account of Shem, Ham and Japheth, Noah's sons, who themselves had sons after the flood*
> [2]*The sons of Japheth...*
> [6]*The sons of Ham:*
>   *Cush, Mizraim, Put and Canaan....*
> [15]*Canaan was the father of*
>   *Sidon his firstborn, and of the Hittites,*
>   [16]*Jebusites, Amorites, Girgashites,*
>   [17]*Hivites, Arkites, Sinites,* [18]*Arvadites,*
>   *Zemarites and Hamathites.*
> *Later the Canaanite clans scattered* [19]*and the borders of Canaan reached from Sidon toward Gerar as far as Gaza, and then toward Sodom, Gomorrah, Admah and Zeboiim, as far as Lasha...*
> [21]*Sons were also born to Shem....*
> [32]*These are the clans of Noah's sons, according to their lines of descent, within their nations. From these the nations spread out over the earth after the flood.*

The Table of Nations

This genealogical and geographical table is called the "Table of Nations." It has been simplified above, focusing especially on the land of Canaan (see 10:15-19). That's because (a) these are the people Israel had to deal with early in her history, the other peoples becoming more significant later in the Old Testament,[18] and (b) it puts Noah's curse on Canaan in sharper perspective. The Jews going into Canaan hearing Genesis 9 and 10 read out loud would have been strengthened in their conviction to fulfill their mission to eradicate the Canaanites and claim the Promised Land.

Here begins the fourth of the Generations (*toledoth*) passages. Remember, the book of Genesis is constructed around ten such passages using the word "account" (NIV) or "generations" (NAS). Several remarks about this genealogical table:

- Many of the men mentioned are also actual *nations* (Cush, Mizraim, Put and Canaan, for example, in 10:6). This is one more reason to be cautious in interpreting genealogies; a name doesn't necessarily mean a person.
- All these peoples and patriarchs lived in the Eastern Mediterranean region, at the intersection of Europe, Africa and Asia.[19]
- Chronologically Chapter 10 *follows* Chapter 11, since the nations are said to have acquired their own languages (10:5, 20, 31) This did not happen until 11:9!
- The Hamites (Egyptians) and Canaanites were peoples who troubled the Israelites in the earlier era of Old Testament history. That is, they are the ones God used to chasten Israel. These names may mean little to us, but they were *full* of meaning for the Jews who read this part of Genesis![20]
- The "earth" over which the offspring of Noah spread out southwards was the area within 1000 miles of the mountains of Ararat.

- The Table, inserted the chapter before the birth of Abraham, spiritual father of the Jewish people, served as a reminder that God loves the Gentiles too—that he had purposes for them as well. Israel did not drop down out of heaven, but was taken right out of the heart of these heathen nations.[21]

Conclusion

Disciples also have their own "Table of Nations." Nations being evangelized, churches planting new churches planting even more churches. Generation after generation after generation of Christians carrying the torch of the gospel. We have one common goal: to evangelize the world. But instead of aiming to spread out over the earth after the flood (9:7), we aim to spread out over the earth *before* the fire.

In our final chapter we will see the state the world got into once again, the incident at Babel, and how God embraced humanity anew and gave them a fresh start, his big heart ever extending hope to those needing it.

Notes

1. Groups such as the "Hare Krishnas" and the Seventh Day Adventists pull verses out of context to support their vegetarian doctrine.

2. Leviticus 3:17, 7:26-27, 17:12-14, 19:26. God's medical advice to abstain from blood and fat would certainly go a long way to reduce coronary disease and heart failure. The Bible's medical wisdom stands in stark contrast to the foolishness of contemporary "medical" and magic texts.

3. The pronouncement could be construed to *predict* the death of the murderer (at the hands of the avenger) rather than to *demand* it. However, this does not seem to be the natural reading of the passage.

4. For adultery (Leviticus 20:10), attacking one's parents (Exodus 21:15), bestiality (Exodus 22:19; Leviticus 20:15), homicide by reason of neglect [the bull goring] (Exodus 21:29), contempt of court (Deuteronomy 17:12), cursing one's parents (Exodus 21:17; Leviticus 20:9), being a rebellious juvenile (Deuteronomy 21:18-21), idolatry (Exodus 22:20; Deuteronomy 13:5, 17:2-5), incest (Leviticus 20:11), kidnapping (Exodus 21:16; Deuteronomy 24:7), being a malicious witness in a capital case (Deuteronomy 19:16-21), manslaughter (Genesis 9:6; Exodus 21:12; Leviticus 24:17; Numbers 35:16), priestly arrogation (Numbers 3:10, 18:7), [female] promiscuity (Deuteronomy 22:21), prophesying presumptuously (Deuteronomy 18:20), Sabbath break-

ing (Numbers 15:35), sodomy (Leviticus 20:13), and sorcery (Exodus 22:18; Leviticus 20:27).

5. The "sword" is the instrument of execution (for beheading).

6. It is not clear whether this was the first rainbow, or whether God adapted the pre-existing rainbow as a sign of the covenant. Circumcision, for example, which became a sign of the Mosaic covenant, had earlier been practiced by many nations, such as the Egyptians.

7. Laurence A Turner, *The Rainbow As the Sign of the Covenant in Genesis XI.11-13* in Vetus Testamentum XLIII, No. 1 (January 1993) 119-122.

8. The fact that this beautiful symbol has been appropriated as an emblem for the gay rights movement and homosexuality in general should not obscure for us its godly meaning.

9. See Habakkuk 2:15. It was Ham's perversity which brought the curse, not his seeing his father's nakedness *per se*. It is tempting to connect this incident with the passages on nakedness and clothing in Genesis 3:7, 3:10 and 3:21, yet the connection is coincidental. 9:22 implies Ham invited his brothers to share in his perversity.

10. Other passages on C_2H_5OH (alcohol): Genesis 9:21; 1 Samuel 25:36; 2 Samuel 11:13; 1 Kings 16:9, 20:16; Micah 2:11; Luke 12:45, 21:34; 1 Corinthians 5:11, 10:21; 1 Thessalonians 5:7; 1 Timothy 3:3; Titus 1:7.

11. The Romans, hardly innocent in sexual perversions, were shocked by the immorality of the Phoenicians who lived at Carthage (North Africa). The Phoenicians were the last vestige of the Canaanite race.

12. *Eisegesis* is reading your views into the text; *exegesis* is drawing the true (intended) meaning from the text. Most false doctrine comes from the former.

13. Interestingly, it was through Christian influence that slavery eventually disappeared in the Roman Empire, and through Christian influence yet again it was outlawed in Britain, through the work of Wilberforce and others in the early 1800s. Political leaders often use religion (even the Bible) to manipulate the people and improve their fortunes. In a way Marx was right: "Religion is the opiate of the people."

14. Genesis 10:6

15. Another of many possible examples illustrating the consequences of this unfortunate doctrine is the case of the Mormons. Mormon leaders had always taught the inferiority of blacks. Brigham Young, for example, wrote: "Shall I tell you the law of God in regard to the African race? If the white man who belongs to the chosen seed mixes his blood with the seed of Cain, the penalty, under the law of God, is death on the spot" (*Journal of Discourses, vol. 10, page 110, 1854-1886*). Until June 1978, when a "revelation" came to the Mormon president, Spencer Kimball, Latter Day Saints barred blacks from the priesthood, since they were under the "curse of Ham." Bowing to increasing civil rights pressure, the Mormons conveniently received the "revelation" and changed their policy.

16. Much of the material in this section is taken from an article by the author and Russ Ewell, "Twisting Scripture" that appeared in *UpsideDown* magazine, January 1994.

17. Shem is mentioned first because the Israelites descended from him; he is in the lineage of Jesus Christ.

18. Except for *Mizraim,* or Egypt, with whom the pre-Israelites make contact several times in Genesis.

19. It seems highly unlikely that the Bible teaches all nations, tribes, peoples and languages (Revelation 7:9) descended from Noah's sons. If they did, why is there no mention of Indians, who were known to Old Testament characters, and whose land is occasionally mentioned? What about the aboriginal Australians, who paleontologists and anthropologists say had lived for 40,000 years on that island-continent? (For more on the idea that the flood might not have *literally* destroyed "every living thing on the face of the earth" see endnote 7 in Chapter 14.

20. Later the Babylonians, Assyrians, Greeks and others played a greater role in Israelite history. They are alluded to in 10:4 ("Javan" are the ancient Greeks), 10:10-11 (cities in Assyria and Babylon) and 10:14 (Philistines). A full commentary on Genesis would take each nation in turn and relate it to the flow of history in the Old Testament.

21. Deuteronomy 9:4-6 was a later reminder of this fact, though it seldom had the intended effect.

16
The Infernal Tower
Babel and Beyond

God rescued the family of Noah, their descendants re-populated the drenched world, and they spread out and multiplied. Generation followed generation. They grew strong in numbers, but weak in spirituality. They failed to appreciate God's "re-creative" grace.

The spirit of gratitude after the rescue from the flood gave way in time to a self-assured and humanistic outlook on life. Mankind lost gratitude and became grasping. At Babel he grabbed for the same thing he was really grabbing in Eden: personal autonomy, "freedom," the right to be master of his own destiny. When we understand what man attempted at Babel, it is truly shocking.

> *[11:1]Now the whole world had one language and a common speech. [2]As men moved eastward, they found a plain in Shinar and settled there.*
> *[3]They said to each other, "Come, let's make bricks and bake them thoroughly." They used brick instead of stone, and tar for mortar. [4]Then they said, "Come, let us build ourselves a city, with a tower that reaches to the heavens, so that we may make a name for ourselves and not be scattered over the face of the whole earth."*

Men moved eastward until they came to Babylon (Shinar).[1] People were tired of traveling. Adam had to pack up and leave, an exile. Cain became a fugitive. Noah was carried far away by the surging flood. And now his descendants wandered, seeking security. (If only they all had known the comfort of Psalm 62:1—"My soul finds rest in God alone.")

Shinar, the Old Babylonian Empire, in all its pride, was well known to the ancient Hebrews. The whole world (presumably the world sketched in Genesis 10) had one common language.[2] Unity is a good thing, provided those unified are good people. But this was hardly the situation at Shinar.

Oh, the Towering Feeling

Man had a plan. He had superior construction techniques. Still on the run from God, he wished for security. The Tower of Babel was nothing more than man's monument to his own ego.[3]

Now, personally, I love tall buildings. Whenever I visit a city, I want to go up to the highest point and look out. My first skyscraper was the Empire State Building in New York City. I was eight years old. Now, though a grown man, I have not ceased to be thrilled by tall structures all over the world! Perhaps the most breathtaking views were Toronto's CN Tower, Sydney's Centrepoint and of course the Sears Tower in Chicago. Tall structures are rewarding to build, exhilarating to ascend, and so, so easy to worship.

Don't get the wrong idea; towers aren't evil (though in the Bible they seldom lead to good). But they do exert a certain magic on our minds. In Babel the tower represents the spirit of the world. It's not just a tower, but also a city. The Genesis writer is not commenting on urbanization in general, but the pernicious sort of urbanization (self-aggrandizing empire-building) which leads to the destruction of society because it claims absolute allegiance. No tower, system, state or political allegiance has the right to lay claim to your soul.[4] Our ultimate reference point must not be such a structure; it must be God in heaven.

Citizens of Babel

What was so dangerous about the brewing situation that God had to "come down" and act so dramatically? What sort of citizen was being produced in Shinar?

Haughty (Ezekiel 16:50), humanistic, "liberal" thinkers who flatter themselves "too much to detect or hate" their own sin (Psalm 36:2). Men and women who commit themselves to a sinful course and do not reject what is wrong (Psalm 36:4). "Guilty men, whose own strength is their god" (Habakkuk 1:11). It's a city where people sacrifice family for money, where lust is confused with love, where weekends and vacations are lived for self, where everyone is too busy for "religion."

We too must watch ourselves lest we become humanistic. There is no such thing as a "self-made" person. As Jim McGuiggan put it,

> Here's a business man who thinks he's "self-made." He was taught in a school he didn't found, lives under a democracy he didn't set up, is part of a "free enterprise" system he didn't establish, drives cars he didn't make on roads he couldn't build, uses phones he doesn't understand, sends mail he doesn't deliver, flies in planes he can't pilot, is enabled to succeed by banks, employees *and* the public. *Aside from all that,* he's self-made.
>
> Here's a "self-made" farmer who learned farming from those he didn't teach, sows seeds he didn't make, depends on sunshine, rain and good land which he didn't create, feeds the land minerals he didn't manufacture *and* sells his produce to the public. *Aside from all that,* he's self-made.
>
> Here's a "self-made" Israelite... Here's a "self-made" disciple of Christ... Here's a "self-made" preacher... Here's a "self-made" teacher of philosophy... Here's a "self-made" church...[5]

The "self-made," self-seeking denizens of Babel, where everyone has an opinion; and if you tell them what it should be, they are all happy to change their minds, their wardrobe, their "friends," their morals. Can't you hear the noise of the raucous nightclubs and sleazy discos of Babel?

You see, Babel is the place where "the wicked freely strut about when what is vile is honored among men" (Psalm 12:8). We are tempted to cry out, with David,

> *Help, LORD, for the godly are no more;*
> *the faithful have vanished from among men.*
> *Everyone lies to his neighbor;*
> *their flattering lips speak with deception.*
> *May the Lord cut off all flattering lips*
> *and every boastful tongue (Psalm 12:1-3).*

The tower in Babel must not be completed! The God of love refuses to let man attempt self-destruction again. After the Fall, God had set cherubim in place, flaming swords brandished. At Babel, he confounds the common tongue of mankind and creates division—a sort of quarantine against ourselves.[6]

> [5]*But the LORD came down to see the city and the tower that the men were building.* [6]*The LORD said, "If as one people speaking the same language they have begun to do this, then nothing they plan to do will be impossible for them.* [7]*Come, let us go down and confuse their language so they will not understand each other."*

> [8]*So the LORD scattered them from there over all the earth, and they stopped building the city.*

Once again, God has protected man from himself by frustrating his efforts. Do you have any idea how often God has acted in *your* life to protect you from the consequences of your own folly and sin?

After God's intervention, work on the city ground to a halt. Without clear communication, no great project can be accomplished.

Unity can be a great blessing or a great curse. "United we stand, divided we fall." Unity is fantastic—if our cause is noble and just!

The grand reversal of Babel will be Pentecost (Acts 2): The scattered nations and manifold tongues of mankind will one day be united, communication will be clear and purpose will be pure. There is hope!

> [9] *That is why it was called Babel—because there the LORD confused the language of the whole world. From there the LORD scattered them over the face of the whole earth.*

Here there is a play on the Hebrew word Babel[7] ("gate of god"). It is now connected with *balal*, the verb "to confuse." What a slam![8] They are really "babbling" now; their message is "blah blah blah." In the consistent style of Genesis, heathen notions and names are modified and thrown back in the face of paganism.

Taking It Beyond Babel

Let's take the practical lessons of this chapter "beyond" Babel—to London, Mexico City, Johannesburg, Manila, Washington, Sydney, Singapore, Miami, Vancouver, wherever we live—and then apply them to our lives.

- Do we hunger for honor and recognition? Do we seek to make a name for ourselves?
- Are we easily flattered? Do we feel ourselves influenced by the "sophisticated"?
- Do we cringe when someone else gets the credit for something we have done?
- Are we more likely to follow God's commandments when others are watching?
- Are we more impressed with degrees and qualifications or character and faithfulness?
- Are we more impressed by *who* somebody knows or *what* he knows?
- Which do we know more thoroughly: radio song lyrics

and sports stats or the Word?

- Are we false optimists? Confident the future will be better because we have "plans"?
- Do we seek security in neat systems?[9] Or in our relationship with God?
- Is God our "tower"—the biggest, most exciting, most impressive part of our lives?

The Infernal Tower

Babel was the infernal tower. Its ego was inflated so large that its field of vision was totally blocked; it did not see God, arms outstretched, pleading. In unmitigated pride it embodied the spirit of the age, having forgotten the truth about the past and refusing to consider the truth about the future. It promised everything, but delivered nothing. In pretense it reached toward the heavens, but its true foundations were in hell.

Don't stand too close to towers like that!

Is It As Hopeless As It Seems?

Mankind's track record is not very impressive from chapter 3 to 11 of Genesis! If you are wondering whether, after Babel, there is really any hope, do not let your hearts be troubled: Grace will be extended in chapter 12. Through Abram (Abraham) God's incredible spiritual blessings will come to all nations—exactly what the confused nations of Genesis 10 needed after the debacle at Shinar in Genesis 11. The theme of grace, so pivotal in the Old Testament, shines through intensely in Genesis.

Notes

1. The word "eastward" is helpful because it gives us geographical information. Man moved southeast from the Ararat region of Turkey. Once again, the easterly component of the vector is less than the other direction involved: south. (This is similar to 2:8.)

2. For more on the intriguing subject of the relationships among the languages of the world, see the book *In Search of the Indo-Europeans,* J.P. Mallory,

NY: Thames and Hudson, 1991. In the author's view it is extremely difficult—if not impossible—to prove that all modern languages are descended from the one language spoken at Babel. Certainly the languages spoken today in the geographical area described in Genesis 10 can be proved to be related: for example, Arabic, Hebrew, Aramaic and Amharic are all closely related.

3. This was one of the Ziggurats (stepped pyramids) discovered at Babylon—possibly the great stepped pyramid of Etemenanki. Ziggurats were topped with pagan temples. (Like the Tower of Shechem in Judges 9:46.) Babylonian religion was heavily focused on astrology; this is the Genesis writer's assault on idolatry.

The *Enuma Elish* (the creation account of the Babylonians) ends with the construction of the temple of Marduk. So it is with the Genesis account: The narrative stretches from Creation to Babel—now exposed for what it is! The implications of the many allusions to paganism in the pages of Genesis are easily overlooked by the modern Western reader!

4. The basic unit of society is the family. Above all places, it is in the family that we must strive for closeness and right relationships. Lose sight of that fact, and everything begins to putrefy. This rules out totalitarianism: Precisely because the state is *not* the basic unit of society, it cannot possibly claim us as its property, for if it does, the true kernel of society will rot and the canker will spread.

5. Jim McGuiggan, *Genesis and Us,* p. 94, Fort Worth: Star Bible Publications, 1988.

6. For some reason, in the Scriptures *tower,* used metaphorically, may be good (Psalm 61:3; Proverbs 18:10), but literal towers more often than not spell trouble. Consider the following locations with references and lessons: (1) Babel, Genesis 11:1-9—don't put your hope in a grandiose city or system. Watch out, don't build monuments to your own ego. (2) Peniel, Judges 8:9, 17— support those who are fighting in a great cause. Don't be apathetic, and don't be cynical. (3) Shechem, Judges 9:49—be grateful to the person who saved you. Pick the right leader to follow. (4) Thebez, Judges 9:51—don't get too close to a strong tower where your enemies are waiting to kill you! (5) Tyre, Ezekiel 26:4—don't scoff, gloat or flatter yourself when the people of God go through hard times. (6) Siloam, Luke 13:4—"Time and chance" happen to us all. Better change now, before something bad takes away your chance. (7) discipleship, Luke 14:28-30—don't start building a tower unless you really intend to finish. There's no other way to be Jesus' disciple.

7. *Bâb-ili* in the Akkadian original.

8. Humorously, *Babel* in my lexicon is located between the word for "stinking things" and the word for "act treacherously"!

9. What about ideological or political arrogance? Did we ever think totalitarianism was a good idea? "Enlightened" leaders making all the important decisions for the people who, after all, are just "children"?

CONCLUSION

CONCLUSION
Who Dares Wins!

A Heart Check

In exploring Genesis, we have dared to gaze upon the heart of God and feel his pulse. The daring heartbeat of our Creator was unmistakable in the pages of the first eleven chapters. Now is the time for a shift in focus. We conclude the book by taking an honest look at our own hearts. Seven prying questions will be asked. It will take courage and objectivity to respond to them—if you dare.

1. Do we *dare to think,* to overcome mental sluggishness and focus our energies on important and eternal issues? God gave us brains, and he meant for us to use them! This book was written to stimulate thought, to make us fall in love with God's word again. Are you thinking, or are you a spiritual zombie?

2. Do we *dare to study,* to delve, to go deeper with each passing year than we ever have before? Or will we settle for "average" in our quest for truth and personal Bible study? Those easily satisfied by the diversions of the world lack the maturity and appetite for serious study. Would you be described as one who studies intensively, eagerly?

3. Do we *dare to take a stand* when we come across new truth, regardless of the implications? Regardless of the inconve-

nience it may cause? Study is useless if we have already decided never to deviate from the mean or upset the status quo. The only one you should be looking to for approval of your thoughts and ideas is in heaven.

4. Do we *dare to change?* Change is rewarding, stagnation so disheartening. As disciples, we don't just take a stand every few years, but rather, every day (Luke 9:23). Either we go forward, or we go backward. The man or woman whose heart is in tune with God's heart is changing all the time. How much have you changed in the last six months?

5. Do we *dare to create?* God is a Creator God, and in one sense only God can create. Only God can make something from nothing. And yet, in another sense, being made in his image means we share in his creativity. It is not God-like to lack initiative or to fail to live dynamically. "What do I add?" and "What difference does my being there make?" are concerns we should have every time we walk into a room of people. At work, in class, at home, out and about—creativity is a decision. Are you creative? Moreover, when our plans go awry, do we dare to "re-create"—to set new goals and chart a new course?

6. Do we *dare to care for people?* Life is primarily about relationships. If we prefer solitude to society, we have numbed ourselves to those around us. They have become less than human to us, because we have declined to honor them as God created them. We are all created to be "people-persons." This will show on a daily basis in how giving we are, in our friendliness, in our active care for the needy and the lost.

7. Finally, do we *dare to surrender everything to God?* He has revealed how badly he wants a close relationship with us.

In Genesis he shows us that even when we fail to show appreciation or consistency or enthusiasm for him, he extends grace and offers a second chance. The question is not, "Does anyone in the universe care about me?" He clearly does! The only response is to gratefully and graciously surrender everything to our Lord. The ball is in your court.

Have you responded to these questions? Honestly? Then you have learned something about yourself. The heart of God is awesome; what about your heart? Are you a man or woman who dares? For "Who Dares Wins"![1]

Notes

1. The motto of the S.A.S., the British Strategic Air Service.

APPENDIXES

APPENDIX A
Genesis for All It's Worth

Now that you have finished the book, what is the best strategy to draw the maximum benefit from Genesis each time you read it in future? If you chose the "fast track" on your first reading, it may be helpful to go deeper in your study of Genesis in your second reading by including what you skipped over. The footnotes contain many ideas and suggestions for further reading. Then this appendix will give you perspective, practicals and preferences in Bible versions to help you in further study.

Perspective

To begin with, always keep in mind that Genesis is the introduction to God's word. Many things laid out here are assumed later in the Bible. When you continue on to Exodus, which ushers you into the legal section of the Pentateuch, remember what you learned about the character of God and his dealings with people. The Law makes so much more sense once you know the heart of the Lawgiver.

As you study Genesis on your own, take care not to read simply to justify your own preconceived ideas. (Have you never done this? Of course you have!) People who are determined to read the Bible *one way* usually succeed in "finding" verses that back up their view. On the one hand, don't forget everything you have acquired. On the other hand, don't be so secure in your knowledge that you become unteachable.

Remember, in handling Genesis you are looking into the heart of God, a God who dares to disclose his nature to mankind. When you get a genuine glimpse, retain it. The hours invested in fruitful study will pay off. Apply what you have learned. Don't let insight slip through your fingers; be quick to put the principles into action and experience their power in your own life.

Practicals

1. Read straight through Genesis. Not necessarily at one sitting, but don't read half of it and then forget about it for a year. A good rule of thumb for reading the Bible is *Don't read the Bible straight through, but do read each book straight through.*
2. Get to know the composition and structure of Genesis. For example, its fourfold and tenfold structure, as explained in Chapter 1 of this book. Not a bad idea for other books of the Bible either.
3. Keep your eyes open, be alert, concentrate. If you are not sure you understand what the writer meant, back up and read the section again. Use a dictionary whenever you are uncertain about *any* word. Don't plow forward with an "I sort of get it" mentality.
4. Search for themes and motifs, such as the "minor" themes inventoried in Chapter 1. This will spice up your private study. You may even discover doctrines and emphases you thought were only in the New Testament.
5. Learn practical passages and start using them. In counseling, in evangelism and in teaching you have superb opportunities to consolidate your knowledge. "If you don't use it, you lose it!" For example, here are seven passages to be familiar with:
   • 1:28: The Lord gives mankind the *biological* great commission.
   • 2:24: God reveals his marriage plan.
   • 3:15 and 49:10: The Messianic prophecies of Genesis, not to mention Messianic foreshadowing, such as that occurring in Genesis 22, Mount Moriah.
   • 4:3-14: The folly of self-pity and how to address someone wallowing in it.
   • 12:3 and 15:6: Key verses for comprehending salvation history and obedient faith as the basis of our righteousness.
   • 18-19: Sodom and Gomorrah and other similar accounts which are full of lessons for today.
   • 29:21 and all of chapter 39: Relationships, sexuality and self-control.
6. One way to learn the passages is brute memorization. I prefer learning verse and passage *location.* That is, you may not be able to quote it exactly, but you can find it very quickly because you know which chapter it is in. (If you are going to remember only half a reference, it is much better to forget the verse number than the chapter number.)
7. Focus on relationships! Genesis is a book of relationships, all the way from marriage and family to friendship with the Lord. The

world is generally very poor at relationships, and disciples have much to learn, especially if they have been converted "straight" from the world. The first book of Moses will help us tremendously.

8. Sometime, skim through the New Testament and collect all the citations of the Old Testament you find. Study their original contexts, how they are used, and learn.

9. Don't be afraid to wrestle with the knotty issues: tough questions unbelievers ask, "scientific" questions about Genesis 1-11, your own doubts—any question is a good question. Dig in. Don't glide over the surface; grapple with the text!

10. Do some rewarding outside reading (Appendix F). Pick up an interesting-looking book on Genesis from your local Christian bookstore. (Be wise, though. When it comes to Genesis, there is a lot of rubbish out there! Get recommendations.)

   Read a book on the evolution question. See the sequel volume to this book (when it comes out next year!). One day read a scholarly commentary.

11. It is refreshing to change versions now and again. There is no "inspired" or "official" translation. Each translation has its strengths and weaknesses.

   Strictly speaking, the RSV and the NIV, for example, are not "inspired by God." The Bible is inspired, but not a particular version. Christians believe the *original* manuscripts were inspired. The Hebrew and Greek texts from which fresh translations are made are informed reconstructions based on hundreds—even thousands—of manuscripts. "How much was lost in the transmission?" is invariably asked. Answer: a few words here and there. As for the OT, the text is around 97% certain; the NT text is over 99% certain. Not a bad grade! The uncertainties affect no essential doctrine, and mainly have to do with spelling differences, word inversions, the copying of numbers and matters of style.

Preferred Versions

Reading different translations is a great way to prevent your personal Bible study from becoming stale. I enjoy rotating versions; after I have finished one Bible I am unlikely to read the Bible again in the same version, at least for a year or so.

There are many English versions—near 100 at last count! On the next few pages are most of the major ones, the majority of which I have read, and hopefully in this listing you will find one that is right for you.

My personal recommendation for the majority of disciples is to read the whole Bible at least once a year. This is a policy I have followed for more than twenty years—the first ten years, unconsciously, after that time, more deliberately. Regular, vigorous reading is especially important for those who preach and teach.

A. *English Versions*
There are many different English translations available, and they come in varying degrees of difficulty. The chart on the next page may help you to expand the versions with which you are familiar

B. *Ancient languages*
There are three major and eleven minor ancient languages in which the Bible appears.

The minor ones are as follows: Syriac, Coptic, Ethiopic, Arabic, Italic, Gothic, Aramaic, Armenian, Georgian, Nubian and Old Church Slavonic. We will focus more attention on the three major ones:

Greek: The Septuagint (LXX) is the Greek translation of the OT. The main benefit from studying it is the insight it affords into the Greek text of the NT. Moreover, the LXX was *the* Bible of the early church. Reading it gives you an entrance into their world of thought.

Latin: The Latin Vulgate, like the Septuagint, is a translation into a secondary language, since none of the original OT was written in Latin. The Vulgate has historically had a powerful influence on English Bibles, as Latin was the language of choice in the Middle Ages. (For a "new style" Latin Bible, try a software package like *BibleWorks for Windows* by Hermeneutika.)

Hebrew: This is the original language of Genesis and virtually the entire OT. Get a pointed text like *Biblia Hebraica Stuttgartensia.* Nothing beats the Hebrew!

Some readers may be past the years in which, realistically, they are likely to learn an ancient language. This does not mean, however, that we should not encourage some of our young people to study Latin, Greek or Hebrew in high school or college. The Bible scholars of tomorrow are studying the ancient tongues today. But since most do not have expertise in these languages, you will find that "interlinears" are time-savers and convey you quickly into the world of the ancient languages. Be careful, though, not to feel a false sense of mastery of a language. Certain useful tools cannot substitute for a working knowledge of the grammar and vocabulary of the particular language.

Abbreviation/Full name	Comments

Those in the first category are written in simplified English. They are fun now and again but may not keep your attention if you have read the Bible through a few times.

NCV	New Century Version	*These are good versions for*
CEV	Contemporary English Version	*your children to read around*
TEV	Today's English Version (Good News)	*the ages of 8 or 9.*

Those in the next group are written at a higher reading level (for an 11-14 year old).

| NIV | New International Version | *NIV is the preferred version* |
| NLT | New Living Translation | *in the English-speaking world.* |

At a similar level are the following versions, which I have listed separately because they are paraphrases or loose translations. While they are fresh, insightful, colorful and enjoyable for public reading of Scripture, they are unsuitable for serious study.

LB	Living Bible	*Fairly inaccurate.*
TM	The Message	*Lots of fun.*
Phillips	The New Testament in Modern English	*Very good.*

The next category includes revisions of older versions which are stricter translations ("formal equivalence" more than "dynamic equivalence"). They are tougher going than the Bibles listed above, but worth the effort.

NKJV	New King James Version	*All these versions, though*
NAB	New American Bible	*not as stiff as their*
NRSV	New Revised Standard Version	*predecessors, are still fairly*
NASB	New American Standard Bible	*formal.*

Next are older versions and original versions of some Bibles in the previous category.

KJV	King James, or "Authorized," Version	*Very difficult 1600s English.*
REV	Revised English Version	*These three are revisions*
ASV	American Standard Version	*of the King James*
RSV	Revised Standard Version	*Version of 1611.*
AB	American Bible	*Catholic leaning.*

Most difficult are probably the literary translations. They exhibit a high standard of scholarship, and will appeal to those with a college education at the graduate level.

NEB	New English Bible	*Fine but a bit speculative.*
JB	Jerusalem Bible	*Also fine. Dictionary needed.*
Fox	Schocken Bible	*Radical; Hebrew feel.*
	(Pentateuch only, as of 1996)	

C. Modern languages

If you are fluent in another language, it may be refreshing to read the Scriptures in that language. You are likely to see the text from a different perspective—part of which may be caused by your being forced to slow down. Unfortunately, in many languages there is no OT version both contemporary and accurate. It is usually a choice between a century-old version and an inaccurate modern attempt. The NT usually fares much better. The fact is that English readers have produced contemporary versions nearly every generation since the 1880s. The demand for English Bibles, for historical and economical reasons, has typically been higher than the demand for other Bibles in other languages—and the money has always been available for new translations.

Some practical advice: If you are sharing the Scriptures with someone who is only beginning to achieve fluency in English, strongly encourage that person to study the Scriptures in his or her own language. Non-English speakers, studying the Bible with an English speaker to improve their English, will fail to grasp the message of the gospel because their English is not at a level sufficient for the concepts to move their hearts.

D. Final comments

Although it will help you a great deal to "rotate" translations, be sure that when you share the Scriptures with your friends you consistently use a version which is easy to follow. This will help them to become Christians. For similar reasons, do not study the Bible every day in a language in which you are not fluent. It is better to slow your foreign language acquisition speed than to compromise your spiritual growth. Implement the eleven practical suggestions, and always keep the right perspective.

That's how to read Genesis for all it's worth.

APPENDIX B
Science and Religion: Friends or Enemies?

Science and religion are totally incompatible. There's no way you can have maximum intelligence and faith simultaneously; the more you have of one, the less you'll have of the other. At least that's the not-so-subtle message from institutions of higher, lower and middle learning throughout the land.

Today it is widely thought that you can be a scientist, living by the light of reason (in which case there is no room for faith) *or* a religious person, (in which case you can never be a *bona fide* scientist since you have sacrificed huge chunks of your cerebral cortex for the thrill of spiritual fantasy). The two are seen as incompatible; one cannot be both Bible-believing *and* a scientist worth his salt.

It used to be the opposite. Science was founded on biblical principles, and all scientists believed in a rational God. Since a rational God would have created a rational universe, the laws of the universe were knowable. During this period called the Enlightenment, it was considered ludicrous to think that the universe, as immense and complex as it seemed to be, was the product of chance (as modern scientific theories assume).[1] And anyone who rejected God as the Creator was suspected of not having all his marbles in his head!

The "divorce" between science and religion is fairly recent. As we are seeing, it was never a valid divorce. Those who imagine the two partners are not free to "renew their vows" unwittingly adulterate their thinking, their relationships, even their scientific publications.

Bible = Science Textbook?

The Bible is not a science book. To insist that it be used as such is a violation of its principal purpose. A telephone book contains many words, and they are arranged alphabetically, but the telephone book was never meant to be used as a dictionary. And if you want to order a pizza, don't waste your time searching in the Ps in the dictionary. Many religious people think that the Bible is a treasure-trove of scientific facts. This is a misuse of the Scriptures. When the Bible does touch on matters of science, geography, history, medicine and other topics, it is accurate, yet it seldom makes direct scientific statements. There are a few exceptions, though, such as the water cycle (evaporation followed by precipitation), understood by science only in the 1800s. Amos 5:8 and Job 36:27 accurately describe the cycle. Perhaps the most striking instances of the Bible's scientific insight are found in the medical portions of the books from Exodus to Deuteronomy, which contain numerous principles neither understood nor implemented until fairly recently in the history of science.

The Bible tells us the *why* more than the *how*. Since it is written for all people to read and understand, it is composed in a simple, down-to-earth style. For example, the words *sunrise* and *sunset* are often used, even though *technically speaking* they are inaccurate. Yet even the newspaper and the weatherman say "sunrise." Have you ever heard the weatherman correct himself: "Actually, this evening at 18:22 Greenwich Mean Time the anti-clockwise rotation of the earth, causing the terrestrial horizon to eclipse the solar body, will produce a sunset effect in the western zone of the troposphere relative to the observer at sea level. Furthermore, let me reassure you that the sun, in relation to the earth, will be going nowhere!"? Of course you haven't!

The Bible is written for us to understand. It isn't scientific as such, but that doesn't mean it's inaccurate. Every word of God is flawless (Proverbs 30:5). It is important to remember that the Scriptures are written *phenomenologically*. This means they describe phenomena as they *appear* rather than as they actually *are*. Some examples of phenomenological descriptions: sunrise (Mark 16.2); rabbits chewing the cud (Leviticus 11:6), whereas actually they practice refection; and bats being included with the birds (Leviticus 11:19), whereas they are, zoologically speaking, flying mammals.

Imagine if the Bible *were* a science textbook: God would be obligated to explain biology, chemistry and physics exhaustively. An Einstein's head would swim. Here are some reasons I am glad the Bible is not a science book:

- It would be very, very long. Millions of pages of articles, books, lectures and lab reports of a scientific nature have been published. If God had made his word scientifically comprehensive—including all aspects of scientific truth—you would need a crane to lift your Bible.

- It would encourage the confused notion that "scientific truth" is synonymous with "truth"—that all truth must be scientific, or it isn't truth. This is manifestly false! Science deals only with quantifiable phenomena. It has nothing to say about such intangibles as love and justice. Even if scientists one day can explain the neurochemistry of falling in love, all they will have done is to describe it from the physical perspective. This no more rationalizes the phenomenon than analyzing a symphony of Beethoven in terms of acoustical physics and music theory "explains" the symphony. The whole is much, much greater than the sum of the parts.

- No one would have been able to understand it at the time it was written. Those poor Hebrews 3500 years ago—what chance would they have had to follow Genesis 1?

- No one today would be able to understand it, either, since the frontiers of science are always being pushed back. What may be widely understood in fifty years may be beyond the present capacity of today's Nobel Prize winners to comprehend!

- The central message (about God and man) would be lost. We humans are designed for relationships: with God, with our family members, with one another. Technological innovations have no doubt made our lives more comfortable physically—who would ever want to return to the days before anesthesia? But mankind is no more happy emotionally than he was at the dawn of human history. Science must be seen in perspective, not worshiped or trusted in as some sort of savior.

Okay, it's not a science textbook. But how come so many things are never mentioned? Why does the Bible never mention the mechanisms of photosynthesis, or subatomic particles, or inert gases like neon, argon, krypton, radon and xenon? Does this mean the Bible has lost some of its relevance? Not at all. In the Bible, God sticks to his subject, which is people: our origin and destiny, relationships, duty and happiness.

Flat Earth?

When the nature of the Bible is ignored or misunderstood, the result is often extreme interpretations. For example, believe it or not, there is a group of religious persons in America who have formed the Flat Earth Society, insisting that the earth is flat and believing that we should take passages like Job 38:13 and Revelation 7:1 literally. They sincerely believe that all "scientific" evidence to the contrary is part of a grand conspiracy fabricated in Hollywood! The problem is that they are "flat" wrong!

Some ancient people held to the idea of a flat earth, while others believed that we do in fact live on "this terrestrial ball." At any rate, there is no way to prove that the Bible teaches that the earth is flat. The conclusion of the matter is that the Bible used terminology contemporary people could readily understand, without making a point of teaching cosmology, astronomy or geology! By the way, the often heard statement that Jesus implied the sphericity of the earth in Luke 17:34-35 is fallacious. The parallel passages in Luke 19 and Luke 21 show that Jesus is speaking of the destruction of Jerusalem in 70 A.D. (his "coming" in judgment), not the end of the world. Nor does Isaiah 40:22, which mentions "the circle of the earth," prove its sphericity. A circle is two-dimensional, not three-dimensional.

Brontosaurus Rex?

Is it Brontosaurus Rex? Of course not! No self-respecting kindergartner would confuse *Brontosaurus* with *T. Rex!* Everybody knows Brontosaurus was a plant-eater, and Tyrannosaurus Rex was the vicious meat-eater. Few topics have generated more interest in recent years than dinosaurs. "Dino fever" has been raging for several decades now, with no sign of letting up!

So why are dinosaurs not mentioned in the Bible? (Or are they?) Does the Bible give us any information?

Let me state clearly at the outset that I believe that dinosaurs really existed. I do not claim, as some religious people do, that God put certain "fossils" in the ground to confound the atheists, knowing all along that this would only serve to harden their hearts! Dinosaurs lived for millions of years, and mysteriously vanished some 65 million years ago at the close of the Cretaceous period. To insist that they died in the Flood is both unnecessary and highly improbable. Unnecessary because they became extinct long before the time of Noah. Highly improbably because the hydraulics of flooding would have left their bodies at the *bottom* of the geologic column, as the heaviest objects. Yet dinosaur fossils are actually found in the midsection of the column! The lower strata are filled with the fossils of simple organisms and (at a higher level) prehistoric shellfish.

Why the waste? For one, the fact is that many species and genera that have existed on the face of the earth are now extinct, and every year thousands more become extinct. Extinction seems to be the rule, not the exception! But ancient plants and animals now extinct did not go to "waste"! Not only have their constituent chemicals been recycled in the "circle of life," but also many of them, under millions of pounds of pressure and over millions of years, have been converted into highly useful organic substance fuel. Ever heard of "fossil fuels"? Next cold winter's night when you thank God for heating, remember that you owe a small debt to some ancient *Brachiosaurus, Pteranodon* or maybe even *Tyrannosaurus Rex* (not to mention millions of tons of other animal and vegetable matter which was converted into fossil fuel)!

Dinosaurs are not in fact mentioned *anywhere* in the Bible! The descriptions of Leviathan in Job 41 refer to the crocodile, not dinosaurs. (Remembering that chapters 3:1 to 42:6 of Job are poetry will help us not to read too much into the text.) No, they aren't mentioned, but then neither is DNA, or the planet Neptune. Of what benefit would that have been to mankind, especially for Israelites living thousands of years ago?

Is there any chance dinosaurs and humans were contemporaries? There is no evidence they were, and this is not surprising, since humans have been on the earth a minuscule length of time, geologically speaking. Now if we take the creation days as literal days, dinosaurs were created just hours before human beings, and they must have coexisted. There is no need to accept this strained interpretation. My research leads me to believe that dinosaurs definitely did not live at the same time as human beings! As for the matter of cavemen, see Appendix D.

There are many topics the Bible never touches on. When Christians say that the Bible is true and complete, we certainly don't mean it *completely* contains *all* truth on *every* subject! A distinct feature of the Bible is its conciseness and brevity. Quite simply, unnecessary subjects are skipped. The message is still relevant to our society—the principles of relationships never change, whereas the consensus of scientific thought is ever in flux. But there's no need to "park" on this Jurassic theme any longer. Back to the subject!

Scientific Facts in Genesis

Even though Genesis isn't a science book, it does contain a few scientific facts:

- *Definite beginning.* Until the 1960s, many scientists still held to the possibility that the universe had always existed. The work of astronomers has now proved conclusively that this is impossible. In short, the universe had a starting point, just as Genesis affirms.
- *Beginning not by chance.* There are many obvious design features in the creation, and a random (chance) beginning cannot adequately account for this.
- *Structure and order.* Scientists speak of "laws" which describe empirical reality. God's word teaches that God is a God of order; the cosmos is not meaningless (as modern man increasingly suspects), but directed and fraught with purpose. After all, modern science is the child of biblical religion! During the Renaissance and afterwards scientists went forward in the conviction that a rational God had created the universe and established the laws by which it was run. Their implicit faith in God was the foundation for their investigations. But later the scientific community forgot its foundation, so to speak, by spurning the God of the universe and his word, seeking instead naturalistic explanations for everything from biology to psychology. This isn't to say all scientists are atheists! (Any more than to say all atheists are scientific!) This perspective is the foundation of modern science, and in accord with all the facts.[2]
- *Original conditions on earth not suitable for life.* God had to create the right conditions.
- *Orderly progress or progression.* God started small and simple and worked up from there.
- *There are certain limits of reproduction.* For example, no matter how often dogs are crossbred, only new breeds of dog-like animals are produced—never a cat-like animal.
- *Man the apex of creation.* Man is no insignificant creature, as mythology and many religions teach. He isn't an afterthought; rather, he is the apex of God's creative work. And the more ground biologists cover, the more proof comes to light that man is complex beyond understanding—unique in the universe. Put into religious terms, there is no need for man and woman to be insecure; we have a purpose, we are both valuable and valued.
- *The "seed" of woman.* Ancient peoples often believed that the *male* made the real contribution in conception; the female only pro-

vided a moist environment in which the seed could grow. But Genesis 3:15 speaks of "seed" of *woman*. In the NIV the Hebrew *zera'* is translated "offspring" in 3:15 and "kinds" in 7:3. Nevertheless, the Hebrew word means "seed," and comes from the verb *zara'*, meaning "to sow or scatter seed." The original "seed" is clearer in a stricter translation. (See Appendix A for the various types of English Bible versions.) With the improvements in the optics of microscopes[3] around a century ago, the Bible's insight was finally confirmed scientifically.

• *Dimensions of the ark.* The physical dimensions of Noah's Ark are remarkable! In no other ancient account of the Flood does the boat meet the correct oceangoing specifications! For more on this, see Chapter 14.

There are several other scientific insights in the remainder of Genesis (12-50)—and far more in the remaining books of the Law. They include circumcision (17:10), which we have come to realize significantly lowers the incidence of penile cancer; the timing of the circumcision on the eighth day (17:12), which proves to be wise because the clotting factor is stronger on the eighth day than on the seventh—or, oddly enough, the ninth; and genetic principles (30:37-43), which were at work in Jacob's experiment with Laban's livestock.

Not that the ancient Jews were advanced scientifically. It was at least two millennia after Moses (after the flowering of Arabic science) that astronomers and mathematicians began to make major scientific discoveries and contributions to humanity. Jewish science contemporary with Moses falls far short of the perfection of the medical portions of the Law. For example, the *Embers Papyrus*, dated to 1550 b.c., states, "To prevent hair from turning gray, anoint it with the blood of a black cat which has been boiled in oil, or with the fat of a rattlesnake." About hair loss: "When it falls out, one remedy is to apply a mixture of six fats, namely those of the horse, the hippopotamus, the crocodile, the cat, the snake and the ibex." (I guess "hair clubs" are nothing new.) Others drugs mentioned in the medical papyri are dust of a statue, shell of a beetle, head of an electric eel, guts of a goose, tail of a mouse, hair of a cat, eyes of a pig, toes of a dog and semen of a man. It is remarkable that none of these popular ideas about health "made it into the Bible." God's words are flawless, refined, purified (Psalm 12:6).

Once again, we see that, while the Bible is not a textbook of scientific knowledge, it does speak truly and accurately when it (occasionally) touches on scientific matters. Normally it describes events and phenomena from our perspective; the aim was to be understood. This is in stark contrast to other sacred writings, such as the Qur'an, which are full of scientific (and historical) errors. The Qur'an states that the sun and stars revolve around the earth (21:33). As in the story of "Chicken Little," pieces of the sky may fall, with lethal effect (34:9, 52:44). Shooting stars apparently protect the galaxies from evil spirits (15:18). In Surah 18, *The Cave,* some boys fall asleep in a cave, with their dog. Three hundred years later they awake and leave the cave (18:9-19). And the list goes on...

Has Science Made God Superfluous?

Lurking at the back of the mind of modern man is the suspicion that, given enough time, science will be able to explain anything, and perhaps even to accomplish anything. Who needs a God when people in white coats can explain everything in the whole wide universe (we hope)? This needs to be addressed, since science has regretfully left a bad taste in the mouth of many Bible believers, just as religion has left a bad taste in the mouth of many academics. Two illusions have been sustained:

- *The illusion of complexity.* Since science deals with extremely complicated matters and faith is for simpletons who can grasp only the most simple matters, why force it? Why try to bring faith into the lecture hall? The problem with this illusion is that complexity is also an extremely cogent argument for intelligent design. (For those interested in a presentation of the basic arguments on the layman's level, see my book *True & Reasonable.*[4]) The intellectual intimidation perpetrated in order to enforce agreement is considerable. That intimidation is often accomplished through deliberate obfuscation—throwing out so many facts and possibilities that the reader is left confused and thrown off the track of the subject at hand.
- *The illusion of objectivity.* Science deals with facts, therefore scientists are objective. Atheism is a more intelligent position than theism. So the prevailing view goes. "Why is it that most *educated* people don't believe in the Bible?" it is asked. You might well reply, "Why is it that most *uneducated* people don't believe in the Bible either?" Neither group has sincerely read and understood it. People for the most part parrot what they have heard from others, without seriously investigating matters themselves.

In no way has God been made superfluous. Complexity as well as objectivity come from God; the brain the scientist uses to explore the universe is itself the gift of God. Science must be seen in perspective!

A Positive Attitude Toward Science

Not that the Christian has no use for science. Science is fascinating. Ever since childhood I have loved science. Witnessing the earlier years of the Space Program made astronomy especially exciting. I remember the day I learned light had a specific velocity. I raced home and instructed my younger brother to turn on the flashlight. My aim was to beat the light beam in a foot race! How was I to know that even if I multiplied my speed a million times, still there would be no hope of winning?

The love of science has never left me, and even now as I travel around the world, trying to convince skeptics and unbelievers about the Bible, I enjoy expounding on such topics as *Science and Religion: Friends or Enemies?* and *Evolution: Fact or Fiction?* I subscribe to scientific journals, buy books on biology, paleontology, archeology et cetera, and rush to read the science section of the daily paper. I hope you too are enthusiastic about science and share in the thrill of new discoveries constantly being made. This will help you to keep an open mind and realize the greatness of the One behind all true science.

Friends or Enemies?

In short, the *best* science and *accurate* biblical interpretation do not conflict! When theology conflicts with science, we invariably find bad theology or bad science. Beware also of "pseudoscience." Sometimes it is false religion masquerading as science, other times it is sloppy science manufactured for partisan purposes. An example of poor science with ulterior religious motives is scientific creationism, which holds that the earth is only a few thousand years old, that there is an enormous conspiracy afoot among the technocrats to suppress the evidence and sustain the illusion that life evolved without God. Though we may regard the majority of these people as being well-meaning, their brand of science is shoddy. Many reasonable non-believers have been turned off to the Christian faith because of their specious arguments. Moreover, their belief that true Christians must follow only their interpretation, which has de facto become a cardinal doctrine (as opposed to the peripheral doctrine which it is and ought to be), is severely misguided.

Bible believers certainly have no cause to feel threatened by scientists. Many in fact *are* scientists. We can all share in the thrill of new discoveries.

Science and religion are not only friends; they are bosom buddies. Solid science is merely retracing the footsteps of God. If in Genesis we are reading about the heart of God, in science we are "reading" the mind of God. Or, as Solomon (quite a botanist and zoologist in his own right—1 Kings 4:33) rightly remarked, "It is the glory of God to conceal a matter; to search out a matter is the glory of kings" (Proverbs 25:2).

Notes

1. With recent advances in astrophysics (on the macro scale of study) and quantum physics (on the micro scale), as well as strides in microbiology, genetics and many other ultracomplex fields, it is a fair guess that the cosmos appears to be *millions* of times more complex now, at the turn of the millennium, than it did at the turn of the last century! The deeper we probe, the more stunning the intricate mechanisms and systems we discover.

2. Occasionally physicists bring up the Heisenberg Uncertainty Principle as "proof" that there is a randomness to the cosmos. Yet ironically the principle itself makes a *definite* statement about the position and velocity of subatomic particles. The Heisenberg Uncertainty Principle thus shows *certainty,* not uncertainty; it in no way proves the randomness of the natural world.

3. Obviously we do not mean electron microscopes! But Jansen's microscope in the late 16th century and Leeuwenhoek's in the 17th century were not able to focus on such a small feature as the unfertilized ovum.

4. Douglas Jacoby, *True and Reasonable* (Woburn, Mass.: Discipleship Publications International, 1992).

APPENDIX C

Pagans Past and Present

The people of God have always been tempted to compromise with paganism. Oxford has defined a pagan as "one of a nation or community which does not worship the true God; a heathen; a person of heathenish character or habits." In Old Testament times the constant struggle of the Israelites was attraction to the religion and practices first of the Canaanites and later of other peoples. In our time few Christians are allured by Baal and Asherah worship. Molech has lost his appeal.[1] Yet attraction to the world and its pagan approach to life is potent all the same.

Pagans Past

It is not with the prophets that we find the first assaults on paganism. Many features of pagan religion are indirectly attacked as far back as Genesis 1. To begin with, man is shown to have fellowship with his Creator, who desires a personal relationship with him. Pagan gods and goddesses, like the Greek and Roman ones we are familiar with, do not love man.[2] Man's duty to the gods is to offer gifts and sacrifices. The gods exist as cosmic "fix-ups" when humans are in trouble. Religion is how humans control the gods, gain concessions from them, or keep them at bay. This is the heart of paganism.

What a contrast Genesis provides! God made man in his own image, not the other way around. Man is special, not a slave of the gods.

Next, the created world is good. This was hardly the view of pagan religions! Because of the Fall of man (Genesis 3) there is sin in this world run amok, yet the original creation was "very good" (Genesis 1:31).

Dominant Gods of the Mesopotamian Myths

Below are the seven most significant deities in Mesopotamia. (See Henrietta McCall, *Mesopotamian Myths*, London: British Museum, 1990.) Understanding who they are throws Genesis 1 into a new light; the writer is addressing paganism, not just monotheism. It should be noted that most gods had consorts—goddesses with whom they had union and procreated more gods. Sometimes the gods had union with mortals, procreating demigods.

- **Anu** - the creator god and sky god.
- **Ishtar** - goddess of love, sex appeal, and war. The most important goddess in western Asia.
- **Tammuz** - Ishtar's lover. He guaranteed seasonal fertility and is mentioned once in the Bible, in Ezekiel 8:14.
- **Ea (Enki)** - lord of water beneath earth, source of magical knowledge, patron of arts & crafts.
- **Sin** - the moon god. His emblem (crescent moon) has survived in many Islamic flags.
- **Shamash** - the sun god. (See 2 Kings 23:11.) In Malachi 4:2 the Messiah is shown to be the *true* "sun."
- **Adad (Hadad)** - god of weather, storms and rain. Important to agriculture.

While Scripture taught that God is *one*,[3] ancient religions had their own pantheon of gods. Like the fickle divinities of Greco-Roman paganism, there was little in these gods to admire. Pagan gods were capricious, selfish and immoral (Judges 9:13). They were distant (Daniel 2:11), not personal. In general they were nothing more than the powers of nature personified! But like it or not, people "depended" on them, and so polytheism flourished, especially as a corrupt priesthood controlled established religion.

Dominant Gods of Canaan

Following are the top three gods worshiped in Canaan to which the Israelites were attracted. Objectively speaking, Yahweh was not included among the three. In addition to these three, there were numerous other deities,[4] including household gods.[5]

Baal - Canaanite vegetation deity and father of seven storm gods. In Israelite history, more popular than Yahweh (God). See 1 Kings 18:16-40 for the big showdown between the prophets of Baal and the prophet Elijah.[6] Baal means *lords.*

Asherah - Originally Amorite, she was the great mother goddess, mentioned in nine books of the OT. Associated with fertility. Asherah poles were set up by altars to Baal and Yahweh. See 1 Kings 14:22-24.

Molech - Ammonite god of the underworld to whom children were sacrificed. Firstborn children were burned alive. These human sacrifices often took place in the Valley of Ben Hinnom (Gehenna).

Sun and moon are not named directly in Genesis, being called instead "the greater light" and "the lesser light." The Hebrew words *shemesh* (sun) and *sin* (moon) are not used. *Shamash/Shemesh* and *Sin* were deities widely worshiped in the Near East. In the Old Testament we do find the Israelites occasionally struggling with worshiping the heavenly bodies (Ezekiel 8:16; Amos 5:25 LXX). In ancient times, as among the modern superstitious, sun, moon and stars were thought to rule human destiny. Yet there is not a trace of astrology in the Bible. Instead, it is shown to be foolish (Daniel 2:2).

Compare pagan methods of divination with the simplicity of the Lord's guidance: Israel's use of Urim and Thummin, prayer, and God's messages through prophets. Some pagan methods were examination of animal entrails; analysis of patterns created by oil on water and smoke from incense; study of the movements of birds and other animals around city gates or in the temple precincts; and interpretation of celestial and meteorological phenomena.

In Canaanite accounts the great dragon (Rahab, or Timat) was slain, cut in two. The top half became the heavens or sky, the bottom half became the earth. We find no dragon slain in the Genesis account, as in contemporary mythology. (When the dragon is mentioned, the image is turned on its head and used to show the superiority of Yahweh.) Nor is there a fearsome, watery chaos to threaten us, as in the pagan myths. God's Spirit has everything under control!

Next, we find sea and earth reduced to their true state: they are no longer worshiped as primeval mother deities. Most ancient religions had a goddess of the earth as well as a goddess of the sea. Sea and earth are prepared for man's benefit, not to rule over him, terrorize him or prevent him from attaining happiness.

Finally, animals exist to serve man, not to be worshiped by him. What a slap in the face to Egyptian, Babylonian, and, in fact, all pagan religion! We are not to prostrate ourselves before the earth, but to "have dominion over" it, including the animals (Genesis 1:26, KJV).

In short, Genesis cannot be properly understood without some knowledge of contemporary creation stories. (Perhaps the most significant is the Babylonian *Enuma Elish*.) Much of the Old Testament is obscure without specific knowledge of pagan practices and religions with which the Israelites were tempted to struggle. On the one hand, there is a polemic current in Genesis against these religions; on the other, there is the positive statement of faith.

A very useful chapter summarizing the Israelite assimilation to indigenous religious rites is 2 Kings 17. Numerous other gods are named explicitly in the OT. For example, national gods are seen in 2 Kings 17:29 and Jeremiah 2:28, 11:13. Egyptian gods discussed are *Amon*, god of Thebes (hidden powers of nature, represented by a ram) in Jeremiah 46:25 and "all the gods of Egypt" (Exodus 12:12) may have included such prominent Egyptian deities as *Re/Ra* (sun god), *Thoth* (moon, learning and wisdom), *Khons* (moon), *Nut* (sky goddess), *Hapi* (Nile flood), *Maat* (truth, justice and order), *Ptah* (craftsmanship), and *Osiris* (life after death).

Assyrian and Babylonian deities are named explicitly in the Old Testament: *Nisroch* (2 Kings 19:37; Isaiah 37:38), *Rimmon* (2 Kings 5:18), *Nebo* (Isaiah 46:1), *Bel*, or *Marduk* (Isaiah 46:1; Jeremiah 50:2, 51:44). The remaining chapters of Genesis, as well as the four other books of Moses, are difficult to appreciate fully without some understanding of contemporary pagan religion. (For a fairly comprehensive reference work on pagan gods, see Michael Jordan, *Encyclopedia of Gods: Over 2,500 Deities of the World*, New York: Facts on File, 1993.)

Pagans Present

Isn't it interesting that in our post-Christian world more and more neopagans are returning to nature worship, pantheism and the old ways of ignorant paganism? Yet there is a different kind of "paganism" I want to address, and that is the cynical, worldly disbelief of some professional critics of the Bible.

The average Bible reader is not aware of the teachings and influence ("yeast") of liberal critics of the Bible. Few men and women graduate from a liberal seminary education without having their faith severely shaken, if not annihilated. Some of the false teachings of these critics are included below.

Mythology

The wonders and miracles of Genesis are considered to be fabricated. The Creation account is mythological and historically inaccurate. No "flood" ever happened. Look for a religious meaning in a miracle story, but don't waste time trying to show it could have actually happened.

We see consistently a serious predisposition to disbelieve any passage with even a trace of the miraculous in it.

God

Enlightened thinkers know that the God of the New Testament is not the same tribal-deity-become-national-God of which we read in the Old Testament. Genesis and other books certainly do not give us accurate information about God. All they tell us for sure is what men believed about God—and that is what really counts. It's not what is true that theologians should be studying, but rather the varying opinions men have about what is true—true "for them."

Truth

In the view of many theologians, truth is totally relative. Absolutes are for the individual to establish. Under no circumstances should person A try to "convert" person B to person A's religion. We are all equally entitled to our opinions. Who is to say what is right and wrong?—such is implied.

Mosaic Authorship of the Pentateuch

The Books of Moses have "mosaic" authorship. Not Mosaic in that they pertain to Moses (one definition of "Mosaic"), but "mosaic" because it is believed that they were written and rewritten by different authors with conflicting theologies. The Pentateuch is a patchwork, in effect. One author, the Yahwist, contributed the 'J' source. He represented the viewpoint of the southern part if Israel, Judah. The Elohist, on the other hand, represented the north of Israel, and contributed the layer called 'E'. Then the Deuteronomist, working in the late seventh century B.C., gave us 'D', the "long lost" book of Deuteronomy. Finally the Priestly writer, editing in the time of Ezra (fifth century B.C.), rewrote Genesis-Numbers yet again, leaving us 'P'. The distinctions are tendentious, and based on alleged and perceived differences in vocabulary and viewpoint, as well as on the different divine names used in Genesis: Yahweh (J) and Elohim (E). (For an adequate refutation of these mistaken notions, see Josh McDowell's *More Evidence That Demands a Verdict,* San Bernardino: Campus Crusade, 1975.)

It is easily seen by the reader of Genesis that *Yahweh* is not used until 2:4, the exact point at which the narrative begins to focus on God's personal relationship with man. Yahweh is his personal name. *Elohim,* on the other hand, specifies his majesty as God. In fact, God has many different names in the Old Testament. To complicate matters for source critics, 'J' and 'E' passages are hopelessly intertwined. Not, in my opinion, because the second editor sabotaged the original text, but because the author used the two names depending on what he wanted to stress about God. Exodus 6:3 brings the two names together and places our interpretation beyond reasonable doubt.

Furthermore, any surface contradictions among the various books of the Bible are left unresolved; little effort is made at harmonization. It is not seen as necessary, because after all, the Bible is the product of man, not God.

The problem is not the view that biblical books have sources. Many books of the Bible certainly do have different layers, or multiple authors, and this is easily demonstrated. The problem is that the word of God is reduced to the word of man (1 Thessalonians 2:13).

Finally, the best scholarship, as well as computer analysis, shows that Genesis has but a single author. ("Computer Points to Single Author for Genesis," *New York Times,* November 8, 1981.)

Morality

Morality—real, objective right and wrong—has given way to "value judgments." We shouldn't "judge" others. Be liberated; accept all forms of behavior—except, of course, religious intolerance. Homosexuality is not sin; it is an alternative life-style which must be safeguarded. We must keep in step with the times.

Inevitably, liberal views of the Bible justify and encourage loose (liberal) morality. Its contribution to the destruction of family life and good character should not be underestimated.

Conclusion

Anyone who disagrees with these indisputable facts is likely to be considered by professors and students alike as naïve, intellectually substandard, or an incorrigible "fundamentalist"—or a combination of the three.[7]

In short, secular thinking has infiltrated our institutions of higher learning, not just in the arts and sciences, but (shockingly) also in Christian studies. Yes, paganism is alive and well!

Notes

1. Though parents routinely "sacrifice" their children to a modern sort of Molech, consigning them to the fires of sin and hopelessness in secular society: immorality, substance abuse, broken relationships, and a deep emptiness which can lead to suicide. How could presumably well-meaning parents in OT times "heartlessly" sacrifice their children? Societal pressure is so strong that few, especially those without the foothold of God's word, are able to resist.

2. The Norse myths present the same scenario, as do the Celtic, Inuit, Mesoamerican and in fact, all pagan religions!

3. Why then does God say "let us" in Genesis 1:26? And is not the Hebrew *'elohim* (god) a plural word? What are Christians to make of this? This may be the "royal plural", as a monarch might say "It is *our* opinion that..." or "It is our greatest pleasure to invite..." And what is the royal court? Possibly the angelic court, who heard and heeded God's commands; otherwise God is deliberating with himself (his Spirit, mentioned earlier). The plural forms in the OT paved the way for later Trinitarian understanding of the godhead. In contemporary cults *plural* forms were used even for *singular* gods. Arguments for polytheism in early Israel based on the plurality of *'elohim* fall to the ground.

4. Such as the Philistine *Dagon* (Judges 16:23-30; 1 Samuel 5:2-7; 1 Chronicles 10:10), the Moabite *Chemosh* (1 Kings 11:7; 2 Kings 23:13), and the Sidonian *Ashtoreth* (Judges 2:13, 10:6; 1 Samuel 7:3-4, 12:10, 31:10; 1 Kings 11:5; 2 Kings 23:13).

5. Genesis 31:19ff; Joshua 24:14.

6. See also 2 Kings 10:18ff; Numbers 25:1ff (!); Judges 2:10ff; 2 Kings 21:9; Jeremiah 2:8, 23-25, 7:9, 19:5, 23:13, 32:29, 35. *Baal-Zebub* is "Lord of the Flies" (2 Kings 1:2, 3, 6, 16).

7. It is not hard to see why I am reluctant to advise many people to attend a (liberal) seminary. Not that seminaries do not have some valuable instruction to offer. But the spiritual climate can be injurious to one's health. To the prospective religion student I ask a few questions:

How many times have you read the whole Bible? If only once or twice, you are not ready for theology school.

How many books a month of a theological nature do you read? If very little, you will not be able to process all the criticisms that will be thrown your way.

How are you doing spiritually, and why do you want to go to seminary?

Read Acts 4:13 and John 7:15.

Evolution and Caveman

Few topics have stirred as much controversy among churchgoers as evolution and the question of our origins and issues related to evolution. Hopefully if you have come this far you have read Appendix B and realize that science and religion are friends, not enemies.

Interestingly, Charles Darwin (1809-1882) was hardly the first to propose the theory of evolution. Some ancient Greeks five centuries before Christ proposed the theory that life evolved from the primordial slime. In Darwin's day many scientists believed in evolution. Even Darwin's grandfather, Erasmus Darwin, wrote about evolution through natural selection in his work *Zoönomia.* What Charles Darwin accomplished where others failed was to propose a mechanism through which evolution might have occurred (natural selection) and then to popularize the theory through his *Origin of Species,* first edition 1859.[1]

Before we commence our brief discussion of a lengthy subject, there are several things to keep in mind.

Initial Considerations

First, the truth about evolution has nothing whatsoever to do with the existence of God. Evolution is an attempt to explain *how* life came to be as it is. Whether God used evolution, instant creation or some other means is irrelevant to his existence. Once again, evolution concerns the mechanisms of life, not the presence or absence of a Creator.

Next, the truth about evolution is not a matter of salvation. I must confess that in my first year or two as a Christian I was convinced quite to the contrary. It was unthinkable that anyone could disagree (with me) on such an obviously important matter and still remain in the grace of God. Christians hold a variety of views on this subject. Even James Orr, whose *The Fundamentals* early this century gave rise to the epithet "fundamentalist," described himself as a theistic evolutionist. If someone does not happen to be in your "camp," you have no right to judge him as unworthy of salvation. There are central, essential biblical teachings, as evident in such passages as Matthew 22:34-40. Theories of biological origins are not included among them! Evolution is a peripheral and nonessential matter.

Third, despite the collective paranoia of many religious people, who are certain that there is a massive conspiracy afoot among all scientists to reject the Bible, this is far from true. There are many Bible-believers among scientists. There is such a thing as bad science, just as there is bad religion; do not overreact.

Fourth, the biological issues are extremely complex. Since the Bible never purports to be a science book, our scientific beliefs should be tempered. The conviction with which we hold them really ought to be in direct proportion to our scientific expertise in the respective area. One does not become a physicist by reading Genesis 1:1-3. In the same way, Genesis 1:11-13 is not the last word on botany! We need to blend humility with courage to embrace truth as we approach matters scientific.

Finally, everyone believes in evolution already. Yes, that's right! The meaning of evolution is "development." The real question is, How does life develop? How much can one life-form develop? Can new species emerge? Can new genera emerge? New families? Where do we draw the line? Did God create a "proto-cat," which then evolved into saber-toothed tigers, lions, and house cats? Or was every species created individually? Did fish really crawl up on the land, or were the first amphibians created independently? The dispute is not really over whether evolution has occurred, but the extent to which it has occurred.

Keep these things in mind. They will prevent your judgment from becoming clouded by personal prejudices or simplistic, convenient ways of thinking.

This appendix is not a comprehensive response to Neo-Darwinism. Time, space and probably your attention span, do not allow for that! All we will do is skim the surface and dig down a bit deeper at a few points. Let's define our terms and draw some conclusions. Finally, we will spend a few moments reflecting on caveman.

Terminology

Eight important terms will be explained. These will not only help you to follow along in the scientific literature, but they will also give you the edge in discussions with those who have never examined the bases of their beliefs (which includes most people).

- *Evolution* literally means "development." The real question isn't whether there is development, but how much development has occurred in the past and is occurring today. Fact: life does develop.
- *Microevolution* is development or evolution on a small scale, as within species or from one species or genus to another. The hard evidence for microevolution is abundant.
- *Macroevolution* is development on a larger scale, as from fish to amphibians, or amphibians to reptiles. The hard evidence for macroevolution is exceedingly slender. In fact, one of the leading evolutionists of our day, Stephen Jay Gould, said "All paleontologists know that the fossil record contains precious little in the way of intermediate forms; transitions between major groups are characteristically abrupt" ("Return of the Hopeful Monster", *Natural History* 86 (6): 22-30, 1977).
- *The Theory of Evolution* states that macroevolution occurs through accumulated microevolutionary changes. Life is assumed to have been generated spontaneously some 3.5 billion years ago. The theory has been extended, and many evolutionists believe that life is likely to have evolved many places throughout the universe, since it happened here. (For a skeptical refutation of the ever-more-popular notion that there is intelligence in outer space, see Robert Naeye's "OK, Where Are They?" in *Astronomy* 37-43, July 1996.)
- *Darwinism* holds that new species have originated through natural selection, which means that nature "selects" the fittest for reproduction and passing on something of themselves (new and improved) to the next generation.
- *Neo-Darwinism* combines Darwinism with modern genetic understanding. If Darwin had understood that biology would become one million times as complex as it was in his day, it is unlikely he would have dared to draw up his theory.
- *Atheistic evolution* holds that evolution occurred apart from the assistance of any god. This must be flatly denied as both against the evidence and mathematically impossible.
- *Theistic evolution* holds that evolution was God's choice of method for the genesis of life and the formation of the entire taxonomic profusion of life forms.

There are several crucial questions atheistic evolutionists have not answered. If they could, we would have to concede to them right away.

Questions for (Atheistic) Evolutionists

1. How did chaos become cosmos? Or, in terms of modern physics, How did the singularity become ordered, stable and dynamic? And what is the origin of complex systems? Complex systems in our cells must have originated all at once in order to function at all. See the thought-provoking article "Planet of the Apes?" by Charles Colson and Nancy Pearcey in *Christianity Today*, August 12, 1996.

2. How did amino acids develop? DNA? RNA? These are astronomically complex!

3. What drives the development of life? Evolutionists often speak of the "life-force." But this is meaningless and smacks of nature worship. Theorizing that some mysterious "life-force" drives life no more explains the mystery of life than positing a "locomotive force" that causes locomotives to move. Nothing has been explained; all that has been done is that a name has been attached to the mystery.

4. How can you prove that one-celled organisms became fishlike creatures? That fish came up on land to become amphibians? That amphibians became reptiles? That reptiles developed into birds and mammals?

5. What is the origin of consciousness?

6. Is morality a biologically or chemically conditioned construct, or do absolute right and wrong truly exist?

7. What makes humans uniquely different from the rest of the animal kingdom?

8. If our brains evolved, like everything else, by pure chance, what reason is there to believe that they apprehend reality with any degree of objectivity? (If

there is a God of order, such as held to by Bible-believers, whose ways are logical and reasonable, there is already a strong reason to believe in the accurate [or at least adequate] functioning of the brain.)

9. Are you aware of the numerous false starts and downright deceptions perpetrated by scientists to advance their interpretations of the development of life on earth? Have you heard, for example, of *Piltdown Man?* This notorious hoax was foisted upon the public and heralded as a triumph for the advancement of knowledge of human evolution. The jaw of an orangutan and the skull of a modern man had been stained and the teeth filed down for the appearance of age. The "fossils" were guarded in a safe in the British Natural History Museum for over forty years from the public and skeptical scientists until 1953. By that time more than 500 books and doctoral theses had been written supporting *Piltdown Man.* Quite simply, there is fraud and exaggeration on *both* sides: scientists' and religionists' alike.

10. Does the fossil record prove your theory, or can it be interpreted in a different way? Does the field of genetics advance your cause, or raise more disturbing questions than you ever imagined were out there?

How would you answer if you were committed to atheistic evolution? Once more, if you believe in theistic evolution, the questions are easily answered by appealing to God. The core biological questions, however, remain. We are asking about two things: How could life evolve by chance, and how has life developed on the planet? Bible-believers of all biological persuasions are united on the first matter, but not on the second.

To say the very least, there are serious difficulties with the belief—

and it does boil down to a certain measure of faith!—that life happened spontaneously. In the old days, spontaneous generation was disproved and discarded. Its comeback has been remarkable, indeed.

Brute Beast or Noblest Creature?

But remember, regardless of how you got here, you are here! What are you doing with your life? Are you acting responsibly? Are you acting more like the "brute beast" you fear may be your ancestor, or like God's noblest creature? If there's a lesson history has taught us, it is the danger of letting science justify immoral actions, of letting it anesthetize us to the pain of the world and dull our conscience.

Caveman

There is incontrovertible evidence that early man (*homo sapiens*) lived in such places as caves. (Now where would you go if you were ejected from Paradise? The Euphrates Hilton?) The fact is, caves make great shelters. Not until Genesis 4 do we read about cities, and later on about metalwork. (The time of transition from the Neolithic period to the Chalcolithic.)

Adam was shorter than we are. In Jesus' day, 5'2" (157 cm) was considered a good height for a man. Many skeletons from the previous millennia are closer to 4'6" tall (137 cm). If he was a Neanderthal (see Question 1 below), his brain was at least 10% larger than an adult male's brain today. Even if he were fully "modern," not having received a command to shave, it is likely that he was quite hairy. He would have had to "make do" with whatever he found outside the Garden. He might not have known how to use a fax machine. Yes, I'm saying that Adam and Eve were most likely "cavepersons"!

Earlier we posed a number of questions to the Neo-Darwinian. Now it's your turn. And so here are a few questions for you about "caveman":

Questions for Bible-Believers

1. Did you know that Neanderthals are human, members of our own species? They are in a different subspecies, taxonomically speaking, *Homo Sapiens Neanderthalensis*, but fully qualify as *Homo Sapiens*.

2. Fossil man's tools were simple, but then all tools were "simple" before the technological revolution. A simpler life-style does not mean simple-mindedness, does it?

3. Is it possible there were "pre-Adamic races"—that is, hominids before the first man, not included in the Adamic covenant? If there

were, how would that affect your faith?

4. Did you know that cavemen buried their dead with funeral ceremonies? That the deceased were often interred with flowers and implements?

5. Since the genealogies of Genesis 5 cannot be used to establish the date of creation, how much does it matter whether people have been on the earth ten thousand, a hundred thousand, or even a million years?

6. What do you know about human paleontology? How many books have you personally read about "caveman"?[2] Do you have any idea what the shifting theories of contemporary anthropologists are? This will help if you are striving to win the heart of a scientist. A good way to keep abreast of the latest theories is to read a few science books each year. Another idea is to subscribe to magazines like *Scientific American*, or more reader-friendly journals like *Natural History* or *Popular Science* (or read them at a local library).

7. Do you know the differences between *Australopithecus Africanus*, *Homo Erectus* and *Homo Sapiens*? Does the name *Dryopithecus* mean anything to you?

8. Did you know that the consensus of anthropologists is that every member of the human race is descended from one couple, based on Cytochrome C studies (in mitochondrial DNA)? Did you know that none believes that man came from apes but instead that both have a common ancestor?

9. How do you view Adam? Could he have been both an historical individual *and* mankind collectively? Does the evidence in Genesis support the specific as well as the generic Adam?

10. How many times have you changed your mind on your interpretation of a part of the Bible? Do you consider yourself open-minded? If you have never changed your mind, it is highly improbable that you are an open-minded person!

Closure

There are multiple benefits to taking time to consider matters scientific, as we have done—albeit lightly—in this appendix and at other points throughout this book. Allow me to enumerate them here:

- Scientific study helps you to answer any lingering questions of your own; it increases security in God's word.
- It is fascinating, and will doubtless increase neural firing in the cerebral cortex. Be thou vanquished, O lazy mind!

- It reminds you of the issues that are central and those which are peripheral.

- It equips you to help unbelievers, who are likely to bring up "scientific" questions, and to do so with credibility, graciousness (Colossians 4:2-6) and a sense of poise.

- It better enables you to appreciate the new frontiers and discoveries in the scientific world, and to evaluate them in the light of sound scriptural principles.

Notes

1. By the way, if you consider yourself scientifically inclined, have you even read the *Origin*? It is stunning how many people glibly refer to books like Darwin's *Origin*, Marx' *Kapital* and *The Bible* without ever having read any of them!

2. E.g., Richard Leakey & Roger Lewin, *Origins Reconsidered* (New York: Doubleday, 1992); Christopher Stringer & Clive Gamble, *In Search of Neanderthals* (New York: Thames & Hudson, 1993); Kathy D. Schick & Nicholas Toth, *Making Silent Stones Speak* (New York: Simon & Schuster, 1993); Donald & Leonora Johanson *Ancestors* (New York: Villard Books, 1994); John Reader, *Missing Links: The Hunt for Earliest Man* (New York: Penguin, 1988); Niles Eldredge, *Reinventing Darwin* (London: Weidenfeld & Nicolson, 1995).

APPENDIX E

What Is Paradise?

"Paradise" has been defined as "the garden of Eden; heaven, the abode of God and his angels and the final abode of the righteous; an intermediate place or state where the departed souls of the righteous await resurrection and the last judgment" (Oxford Dictionary). (The English word "paradise" comes from the Greek *paradeisos,* which in turn derives from the Avestan [Persian] *pairidaeza,* meaning "enclosure." The Hebrew *pardes* is a clear cognate. The basic sense is that of an enclosed garden.)

Is the definition right? Is it really all these things? Is paradise synonymous with heaven? All three meanings above can be correct.

Paradise can be used interchangeably with heaven, yet in the Bible it is normally where the departed righteous go *before* being ushered into heaven.

What Happens When We Die?

Few questions are asked by Christians more often than this one. Do our souls sleep? Do they go straight to heaven? Are we aware of what is happening "down" on the earth? While I realize that Christians differ on some of these issues, about which one must not be too dogmatic, it seems profitable to look at several things the Scriptures teach.

Jesus promised the thief that "today" he would be with him in paradise (Luke 23:43). Is "today" a psychological instant? That is, was the penitent thief to be with Jesus in the next moment of consciousness (perhaps thousands of years later)? Or is "today" not chronologically a day as normally understood? Anyway, how could he be with Jesus in paradise when Jesus had not yet ascended to the Father (John 20:17)? Difficult questions all.

The Antechamber to Heaven

To begin with, let's take Jesus at his word, in the simplest understanding of his promise to the thief. That very day, as we mortals reckon time, the thief was to be with Jesus in paradise. This was something very, very good and of which he would be conscious. Paul's use of "asleep" in 1 Corinthians 11:30 and 15:51 is figurative. (It would have been of little encouragement had Jesus said, "Today you will be with me in paradise, but you won't experience anything because you will be asleep.")[1] But where is paradise?

Paradise is no physical place—it isn't anywhere on the earth or out in space. Yet, that does not mean it isn't a real place! It is a *spiritual* place. Paul went there (2 Corinthians 12:4)[2]—and yet, there is no evidence that Paul had died in order to go there. In the parable[3] of the Rich Man and Lazarus the first man was in torment, while the second was in comfort. "Abraham's bosom," to which the angels carried Lazarus as soon as he died, seems to be identical to paradise. Readers often assume that Abraham's bosom and the flames of torment both were the *eternal* destinies of those sent to those places. But the text never says that; we have imported the idea from other passages.

In my view, paradise is the waiting chamber to heaven.[4] In 2 Peter 2:9 we read of the wicked being held and punished *before* the day of judgment! No one is actually ushered into heaven or hell until the judgment day, which has not yet occurred.

Paradise is a place of reward. We will be conscious there. Unless we are taken to be with the Lord in the last generation to live on the earth (1 Thessalonians 4:13-18), we too will spend some time in paradise *before* we go to heaven.

Revelation 2:7 assures us that in paradise we will receive the right to eat from the Tree of Life (Genesis 2:9). Once we have crossed the chasm between the living and the dead, we cannot change our status as far as salvation goes. If we died saved, we will remain that way forever. If we died separated from God, there will be nothing we can do to change that reality. We must face the music.

What Heaven Is Not

All religions have a deep-felt need for a place of reward (a heaven or paradise) as well as a place of punishment.[5] There is something in the spiritual heart of man that knows that he, as a sinner, deserves punishment, while the righteous deserve some reward. This isn't just "salvation by works." It's fair and biblically correct.

Whatever the Bible means by paradise, it is certainly is not the worldly "paradise" of Islam, Hinduism and other religions. In man-made religions, paradise is the place where sin becomes acceptable. In fact, for keeping oneself from sin during his earthly life, one is re-warded with the very sins he abstained from! Consider this well-known citation from the Qur'an:

> The true servants of Allah will be well provided for, feasting on fruit, and honored in gardens of delight. Reclining face to face upon soft couches, they shall be served with a goblet filled at a gushing fountain…delightful to those who drink it.…They shall sit with bash-ful, dark-eyed virgins,[6] as chaste as the sheltered eggs of ostriches (Surah 37).

This is nothing more than a natural, humanistic way of envision-ing heaven. It is attractive (if you are a man, that is[7]) because it appeals strongly to the ego and the libido.[8] In the same way, the Vikings had their Valhalla, the banquet hall of Odin (Woden), where the Valkyrie maidens waited on the warriors who fought by day and feasted by night.[9]

Secondly, heaven is not a place of lethargy. Even in Eden God had work for man to do (Genesis 2:15). We were created to be busy, to be active, to function with a certain level of pressure and intensity. I per-sonally enjoy hard work, and recreation is never more rewarding than when I know I have been pouring myself out for what I believe is worthwhile. Sports and games, in a similar way, are much more fun when the competition is more intense. Do we really think the corrupt-ing influence of idleness and laziness will somehow be checked in heaven? Is it not more reasonable to suppose that God has something for us to do?

Thirdly, it is not boring! We find ourselves almost forced to come up with colorful analogies to convince ourselves that heaven will not be dull. We imagine a place where we can eat mountains of sumptu-ous foods without expanding the waistline. Or a place where we can fly, accomplish superhuman feats or participate in incredible adven-tures. The more intellectually inclined may conceive of heaven as an infinite library chock-full of scintillating reading. But, in fact, none of these fantasies would be interesting in the slightest, next to the real thing. Most of our questions about life, science, even about Bible pas-sages whose meaning is hidden from us, will probably seem too trivial to bring up when we see the Lord as he really is (1 John 3:2), when we are transformed (Philippians 3:21).

What Heaven Is

Heaven is a reward. It is fellowship with our God. It is a rest, yet there will be plenty to do. All our needs will be met. We will not be troubled—by bad memories, fleshly temptations, nagging doubts, aching muscles. After life on earth, we will be weary, and we will need a break. Heaven will be a fresh start.

The many metaphors in Revelation 21-22 are commonly understood to be describing heaven. Strictly speaking, this passage describes the church triumphant, delivered from the Roman persecution.[10] Yet to get a glimpse of the glory of heaven, it is appropriate to extend these metaphors beyond the time of John and the cessation of persecution to the end of time. It is impossible, in fact, to read Revelation and *not* think of heaven and the new order of things.[11]

Heaven will be magnificent! It is the place where "glory, honor and immortality" (Romans 2:7) will be non-stop elements of our very existence.

Reflections on Paradise

As we let our imaginations run, it is still imperative to keep an eye on the pages of the Bible. Two engaging questions will be presented; contemplate them as you now ponder eternal matters. I do admit that the following thoughts are somewhat speculative; hopefully these questions will, if nothing else, spur you on to hammer out your own beliefs.

How Literal Is Eden?

Most readers of this book (including me!) understand Eden to be a literal place, and try to take as many details of the account of Adam and Eve literally as we can. Yet when it comes to "paradise" at the other end of the Bible (Revelation 21-22), most of us take the details as symbolic. Why not the other way around? Why not take Revelation as literal and (early) Genesis as symbolic—as Ezekiel 28:13 does? Even the apostle John fuses Genesis 2 with the imagery of Ezekiel 47 in the final chapters of the Apocalypse.

Now I know this may sound like heresy to some of my readers, so it may comfort you to know I am *not* actually suggesting that Genesis 2-3 doesn't describe actual, historical events. Yet could there still not be some elements of symbolism in the account?

There are three basic possibilities regarding Eden and the account of Adam and Eve. They are purely *mythical*—the view of most theologians; they are *literal*—the view of most fundamentalists; or they are *both symbolic and historical*—which is my view.

Adam, Eve, Satan, Eden and so on truly existed, yet the entire Eden account is couched in symbolic language. For a parallel in the New Testament, see Revelation 12, where the woman clothed with the sun is the church, Satan is the dragon, and after the birth of a male child (Christ) the woman is protected in the desert—symbolizing God's faithfulness to his persecuted saints. These details are not literal; any reader must come to grips with what they represent. John is patently describing historical realities in the first century. This is the view of most Christians, who take certain elements more literally than others. I've never read an author who treats *all* the images of the Eden narrative as non-symbolic.

To sum up, in my view, the Eden account gives us *historical realities couched in symbolic language.*[12] Biblically, we find human history is framed between two paradises: paradise lost (early in Genesis) and paradise regained (late in Revelation).[13] In the final paradise, as in the first, mankind will forever no longer be alone. Yes, Adam and Eve truly existed—of course there was a first couple[14]—and they walked for a time in innocence and unbroken fellowship with God. To understand what happened to them, and therefore to us, you have to read the Genesis account. There is no other way to understand accurately the root of our plight and the key to our freedom.

Are the Departed Saved in Paradise or in Heaven?

The second question concerns what happens immediately after death. If no one has ascended into heaven (John 3:13),[15] even a worthy man like David (Acts 2:34), may it not be that all the departed saved are in paradise, waiting—as are the wicked in Tartarus (2 Peter 2:9)—for the Judgment Day?

If so, then true disciples who have died (under both covenants) are being rewarded even as you read this sentence, although they have not yet gone to heaven.

What about the "great cloud of witnesses" already in heaven which Hebrews speaks of? First of all, nowhere does the text (Hebrews 12:1) say that the witnesses are in heaven. Second, the cheering crowd may well be used in a metaphorical sense; can we really infer from this passage that they are watching us and emotionally involved in our struggle? Perhaps they are, perhaps not; but this passage does not give us enough to go on. Even if the great cloud of witnesses is watching us, could they not be doing it *from paradise?* After all, in Luke 16:19-31 those on the saved side of the chasm were somehow aware of those on the damned side.

The simplicity of this understanding is this: Everyone on the planet, the quick and the dead, are judged at the same time. John 5:28-29 informs us that all will be judged on the same day. But how can this be true if the dead saints are already in heaven?[16]

What happens, then? The saved wait in paradise (consciously and happily) as long as the damned wait in Tartarus, which is until the Judgment Day. This judgment is *declarative, not investigative.* God won't be examining the records of our lives to determine, in something like a courtroom scene, whether we "made it." Rather, he'll be declaring what we knew all along: our final destiny. At this point the righteous will be escorted into the glory of heaven, while the wicked will be cast into the lake of fire. Those who loved God will be saved forever, while those who rejected him will be destroyed.[17]

Another Day in Paradise

Paradise: the indescribable, the ineffable (2 Corinthians 12:4). On the one hand, paradise is the antechamber to heaven. Even though we may have to wait, no one will be complaining! On the other hand, it is everything we long for and all God's richest purposes for his children. The twin meanings of "paradise" dance through the pages of Scripture.

Indeed God has set "another day" (Hebrews 4:8), when, in his wisdom, he will bring all mankind before his throne to be pronounced guilty or innocent, and we will *fully* receive what is due us. Those who have dared to walk as Jesus walked (1 John 2:6) will be restored to the pristine purity and the uninterrupted joy of Eden: Eden revisited.

Then we will have the incredible opportunity to speak of "another day in paradise." So think twice!

Notes

1. Sometimes 1 Samuel 28 is held to describe the intermediate state, in which Samuel is "disturbed" (1 Samuel 28:15). There are two reasonable doubts about this theory that lead to our rejecting it as unhelpful to our discussion. First, the witch may not have called up Samuel, but an evil spirit (see 2 Corinthians 11:13). Necromancy, or consulting the dead about the future, was strictly forbidden by the Law (Leviticus 20:27; Deuteronomy 18:10-11). Forces darker than we are able to imagine are involved in the Endor incident. Second, what happened to the dead *before* the ascension, when Jesus "led captivity captive" (Ephesians 4:8 KJV) may not so easily be generalized to the new reality now that Jesus has redeemed the Old Testament saints by his blood and the new covenant has come into effect.

2. It seems to be synonymous with the "third heaven" in the Corinthian passage. Or it may be that paradise, along with other realities, occupies the

space known as the third heaven. In the pseudepigraphal *2 Enoch* the third heaven contains both paradise and hell (2 Enoch 8:1-10:3).

3. I take this as parabolic, for several reasons: It reads and feels like a parable; the name *Lazarus* is symbolic—from the Hebrew *Eleazar,* meaning ("God comforts") (see Luke 16:25); there is no strong theological reason to take it as historical. The medieval church took it literally. Ultimately it does not matter whether this is a parable or not; the spiritual truths are what apply to our lives.

4. If this is too novel for you, let me remind you that Luther (1483-1546), Calvin (1509-1564) and Zwingli (1484-1531), the fathers of the Reformation, all believed in an interim state between death and final judgment.

5. Ironically, Buddhism, which started off as an atheistic world-view, eventually created many heavens and eight or more hells—at the popular level. That is, modern Buddhism in many ways resembles Islam, Catholicism and many other religions in their evolution away from their starting principles. Popular Hinduism, too, has heavens and millions of hells; it seems that even when the intellectual elite of a religion deny the truth, the people often reconstruct it—almost by popular (emotional) demand.

6. Surah 78:29 offers "high-bosomed maidens, whom neither man nor jinnee will have touched before."

7. The Qur'an calls paradise a "band of brothers"! (Surah 15:47)

8. *"Eat and drink till your heart's content,"* Surah 69 says of the oasis of paradise.

9. As one writer put it, "Valhalla was not the only paradise that provided escort services for its male clientele: the Celts had a Land of the Women, medieval Germans had the ambiguous Venusberg, and of course the dark-eyed *houris* of the medieval Muslim paradise are famous." (Alice K. Turner, *The History of Hell,* New York: Harcourt & Brace, 1993, p. 106.

10. If Revelation 21-22 refers primarily to heaven, why does the New Jerusalem come down *out of* heaven? (21:2). Moreover, why are the nations (Gentiles) still on the earth? (21:26). And why do they require healing? (22:3). Who are these people who dwell outside the city of God, anyway? Their kings are said to bring their splendor into the New Jerusalem (21:24). These questions do not go away by our insisting even louder that this passage must be speaking directly of heaven! Indirectly, yes; directly, not necessarily.

11. For some helpful material on the historical context of Revelation, from slightly different perspectives, see Gordon Ferguson's *Mine Eyes Have Seen the Glory,* Woburn, Mass.: Discipleship Publications International, 1996, and Jim McGuiggan's *The Book of Revelation,* Lubbock: Star Publishing, 1978. For a totally different perspective, see Max R. King, *The Spirit of Prophecy,* Warren, Ohio: King, 1971.

12. For an excellent (though heavy-going) work convincingly promoting this view, see Henri Blocher's *In the Beginning: The Opening Chapters of Genesis,* Downers Grove: InterVarsity Press, 1984.

13. Between the indefinite past and the indefinite future is the definite present, the temporal space we occupy and the time in which it is our responsibility to make every effort to influence this world for Jesus Christ.

14. Study of mitochondrial DNA has led some scientists to speak of "Mother

Eve" (see Genesis 3:20), a hypothetical female living somewhere in Africa, according to the common version, no more than 200,000 years ago, and through whom all living humans are descended. Though this is farther back than the Genesis account seems to imply—and it is tricky to judge in this matter!—it is interesting that some biologists are unwittingly taking Genesis 3:20 at face value!

By the way, anthropologists and evolutionists do not generally posit the multiple evolution of man. That is, they believe that lower life forms became man *once,* and *one* stream of evolution flowed from that point.

15. I realize that this situation may have been superseded after the resurrection and ascension of Jesus by a new reality, i.e., Jesus opened a direct entrance into heaven, in some sense "bypassing" the future Judgment.

16. How can this be true without being forced to postulate, for example, some sort of time warp—a *deus ex machina* which saves the interpretation without necessarily being loyal to the face-value meaning of the Scriptures?

17. The notion that the lost have a "second chance" after death is based on one possible interpretation of 1 Peter 3:18-20, which assumes something contradicted by Hebrews 9:27. For an expansion of this doctrine, see my *Life To The Full* (Discipleship Publications International: Woburn, Mass., 1995), Chapter 10. Nor is there reincarnation (Hebrews 9:27; Job 7:9).

APPENDIX F

Rewarding Reading

The purpose of this final appendix is to stimulate the reader to further study. Rather than give an overwhelming list of reading suggestions, I have chosen instead to make only a few suggestions in each category.

As a rule, choose your books as carefully as you choose your friends. I am reluctant to keep a book I do not think is excellent, and have given away (or thrown away!) many, many books. The volumes remaining in my study are reference works I consult frequently, or books I would be proud to lend out.

Aim to average at least a book each month. Read selectively. "Test everything; hold on to the good" (1 Thessalonians 5:21). Take pride in your collection. It is your personal treasury of biblical resources to enrich your study of God's word.

Naturally, full-time ministers are encouraged to read much more, teachers and theologians a minimum of 4 or 5 per month. 2 Timothy 2:15 is an upward call to ministers to deepen their Bible knowledge, and thus to become a channel through which other Christians may benefit from the minister's personal study.

Works on Genesis

- Henri Blocher, *In the Beginning,* Downers Grove, Ill.: InterVarsity Press, 1984.
- Jim McGuiggan, *Genesis and Us,* Fort Worth: Star Bible Publishers, 1988.
- Francis Schaeffer, *Genesis in Space and Time,* Downers Grove, Ill.: InterVarsity Press, 1972.
- Daniel Vestal, *The Doctrine of Creation*, Nashville: Convention Press,

1989.
- John Willis, *Genesis,* Abilene Christian University Press Abilene, Texas: 1993.
- Dr. John Sailhamer, *Genesis Unbound,* Sisters, Oregon: Multnomah Books, 1996.

Introductions to the Old Testament
- Gleason L. Archer, *A Survey of Old Testament Introduction,* Chicago: Moody Press, 1964.
- William Sanford La Sor, David Allen Hubbard, and Frederic William Bush, *Old Testament Survey,* Grand Rapids, Mich.: Eerdmans, 1982.

Helpful tools
- Yohanan Aharoni et al, *The Macmillan Bible Atlas,* New York: Carta, 1993.
- *The Lion Encyclopedia of the Bible,* Tring, England: Lion (Eerdmans, USA), 1978.
- James B. Pritchard, Ed., *The Times Atlas of the Bible,* London: Times Books, 1987.
- W. E. Vine, *Vine's Complete Expository Dictionary of Old and New Testament Words,* New York: Nelson, 1985.

Difficult passages
- Gleason L. Archer, *Encyclopedia of Bible Difficulties,* Grand Rapids: Zondervan, 1982.
- Walter C. Kaiser, *Hard Sayings of the Old Testament,* Downers Grove: InterVarsity Press, 1988.
- Walter C. Kaiser, *More Hard Sayings of the Old Testament,* Downers Grove: InterVarsity Press, 1992.

Works dealing with various aspects of science
- John N. Clayton, *The Source,* South Bend, Ind.: Clayton, 1990.
- Alan Hayward, *Creation and Evolution,* London: Triangle, 1994.
- Phillip E. Johnson, *Darwin on Trial,* Downers Grove: InterVarsity Press, 1990.
- Denton, Michael, *Evolution: A Theory in Crisis,* Bethesda: Adler & Adler, 1985.

OTHER BOOKS FROM
DISCIPLESHIP PUBLICATIONS INTERNATIONAL

The Daily Power Series
Series Editors: Thomas and Sheila Jones

Thirty Days at the Foot of the Cross
A study of the central issue of Christianity

First...the Kingdom
A study of the Sermon on the Mount

The Mission
The inspiring task of the church in every generation

Teach Us to Pray
A study of the most vital of all spiritual disciplines

To Live Is Christ
An interactive study of the Letter to the Philippians

Glory in the Church
God's plan to shine through his church

The Heart of a Champion
Spiritual inspiration from Olympic athletes

Jesus with the People
Encountering the heart and character of Jesus

Practical Exposition Series

Life to the Full
A study of the writings of James, Peter, John and Jude
by Douglas Jacoby

Mine Eyes Have Seen the Glory
The victory of the Lamb in the Book of Revelation
by Gordon Ferguson

Power in Weakness
Second Corinthians and the Ministry of Paul
by Marty Wooten

The Call of the Wise
Introduction and Topical Index to the Book of Proverbs
by G. Steve Kinnard

The Victory of Surrender
An in-depth study of a powerful biblical concept
(workbook and tapes also available)
by Gordon Ferguson

True and Reasonable
Evidences for God in a skeptical world
by Douglas Jacoby

Raising Awesome Kids in Troubled Times
by Sam and Geri Laing

Friends and Lovers
by Sam and Geri Laing

Friends and Lovers Study Guide
by Mitch and Jan Mitchell

Let It Shine: A Devotional Book for Teens
edited by Thomas and Sheila Jones

Mind Change: The Overcomer's Handbook
by Thomas A. Jones

Especially for Women

She Shall Be Called Woman
Volume I: Old Testament Women
Volume II: New Testament Women
edited by Sheila Jones and Linda Brumley

The Fine Art of Hospitality
edited by Sheila Jones
The Fine Art of Hospitality Handbook
edited by Sheila Jones and Betty Dyson
(two-volume set)

Our Beginning: Genesis Through the Eyes of a Woman
by Kay Summers McKean

For information about
ordering these and many other resources from DPI, call toll-free
1-888-DPI-BOOK or from outside the U.S.: 617-938-7396
or write to DPI, One Merrill Street, Woburn, MA 01801-4629
World Wide Web
http://www.dpibooks.com